100+ Literacy Lifesavers

100+ Literacy Lifesavers

A Survival Guide for Librarians and Teachers K–12

Pamela S. Bacon and Tammy K. Bacon

LIBRARIES
UNLIMITED
A Member of the Greenwood Publishing Group

Westport, Connecticut • London

Library of Congress Cataloging-in-Publication Data

Bacon, Pamela S., 1964–
  100+ literacy lifesavers : a survival guide for librarians and teachers K–12 / Pamela S. Bacon
  and Tammy K. Bacon.
      p. cm.
  Includes bibliographical references and index.
  ISBN 978-1-59158-669-2 (alk. paper)
  1. Reading. 2. Teaching teams. 3. School librarian participation in curriculum planning. I. Bacon, Tammy K.
II. Title. III. Title: One hundred plus literacy lifesavers.
LB1573.B235   2009
428.4'071—dc22   2008045514

British Library Cataloguing in Publication Data is available.

Library of Congress Catalog Card Number: 2008045514
ISBN: 978-1-59158-669-2

First published in 2009

Libraries Unlimited, 88 Post Road West, Westport, CT 06881
A Member of the Greenwood Publishing Group, Inc.
www.lu.com

Printed in the United States of America

The paper used in this book complies with the
Permanent Paper Standard issued by the National
Information Standards Organization (Z39.48–1984).

10 9 8 7 6 5 4 3 2 1

This book is dedicated to our friends and families who often wonder what we are doing on our writing retreats. One word: Collaborating!

CONTENTS

Chapter 1:
Surviving Media Center Collaboration

Chapter 2:
Utilizing Different Genres

Chapter 3:
Reading Strategies (Before–During–After)

Chapter 4:
Visualization Activities

Chapter 5:
Implementing Literature Circles

Chapter 6:
Visiting Authors and Author's Purpose

Chapter 7:
Independent Learning and Workstations

Chapter 8:
Needs Assessment, Data, and Rubrics

Chapter 9:
Graphic Organizers

Chapter 10:
Lifesaver Tributes

CONTRIBUTORS

Wendy Auman

Diana Callahan

Anna Cook

Tom Geilfuss

Carl Harvey

Kay Kelley

Gwen Morris

Kelly Rich

Shannon Rose

Nancy Witty

Please note that contact information for the contributors is included in the Tribute chapter of this book (refer to Literacy Lifesavers #91–100).

INTRODUCTION

This book is intended to be used equally by library media specialists and classroom teachers. Both roles are equally important—and critical—to improve ever-increasing literacy needs. Throughout the book, you'll find many "tweaks." Tweaks are provided whenever possible. Tweaks can make a given strategy work for various grade levels. The Literacy Lifesavers that don't include tweaks are usually in professional-development strategies that fit the entire K–12 audience. Some chapters have been divided into primary and secondary strategies for ease of use; therefore, tweaks will be at the discretion of the teacher or media specialist to determine what would best meet the needs of his or her students.

Given the media center's challenging demands, the media center specialist may be unable to get involved in all of these literacy activities. Time constraints simply don't allow it. However, the idea is that these strategies should be used, whenever possible, in collaborative units and co-teaching lessons.

Formatting

This book is unique in that you will recognize two distinct voices and perspectives throughout the text—the voice of the teacher and the voice of the media specialist. This collaborative approach is critical for the teacher and the media specialist to be able to dive into previously uncharted waters while still being able to get their feet wet in their own environments with the different strategies.

The Literary Lifesavers in each chapter are formatted as follows:

Lifesaver Talk: An introduction to each lifesaver in a brief, narrative format.

Lifesaver Tips: Quick lifesaving tips to help you stay afloat.

Lifesaver Tweaks: How to "sea" the lifesaver work at your grade level.

Lifesaver Trips: Internet destinations to visit on your ocean journey.

The book concludes with two additional features:

Lifesaver Tributes: More Literary Lifesavers by a special group of contributors—a travel guide to help you discover other "dive experts."

Lifesaver Texts: Each Tribute includes great text resources for you to "sea," recommended by your dive experts.

Book Outline

LITERACY COLLABORATION

Chapter 1

Surviving Media Center Collaboration

"Sea" Levels: Dive into Collaboration

When the media specialist and classroom teacher collaborate, amazing learning can occur! Sometimes the media specialist is just a little involved (just sticking her big toe in the water); sometimes the media specialist takes the lead (jumping in head first). No matter how involved the media specialist is, planning is the key to smooth waters and high "C"s! Below are the various types of collaborative engagement for each role.

Level 1: One Leads

The lowest level of collaboration (and perhaps the most common) occurs when students are kept in one large group. The teacher leads the group, while the media specialist provides the necessary resource materials.

Level 2: One Leads and One Follows

The lowest level of collaboration occurs when students are kept in one large group. The media specialist must rotate around the classroom or media center while monitoring and keeping the students on task.

Level 3: Alternate Leads (Co-Teaching)

Each partner (teacher and media specialist) has a lead role, but the lead role alternates for a portion of the lesson. It is important that both parties actively monitor the room and provide smooth transitions between lesson parts.

Level 4: Literacy Stations/Student Leads

Students are placed in small, mixed-ability groups. The teacher and media specialist (and any able body) monitor and facilitate the station activities. Both parties are equally involved in planning and resource gathering.

Level 5: Simultaneous Leads

Students are divided into two heterogeneous groups. Both the teacher and media specialist are teaching the skills simultaneously.

Lifesaver Tips

- Ensure that students see both partners as lead teachers. Even at Level 1, students must view the media specialist and the lead teacher as important vessels of knowledge.

- To avoid distractions, the teacher should limit off-task conversation with students who may seek inappropriate attention.

- Both teachers play an active role in monitoring, using proximity to ensure learners are engaged and accountable. No paper grading or e-mail checks during this time!

- When the lead teacher is teaching or presenting, the "follow" teacher may ask questions for clarification or reinforce key points as needed.

- Be prepared to actively model the strategies being taught.

- Extensive co-planning is critical. "Sea" Lifesaver Tool #1 to stay afloat.

- Depending on the level chosen, noise levels may need to be carefully adjusted (i.e., stations and small groups can "sink" a quiet area if not checked).

- Consider placement of stations to keep noise-level distractions to a minimum.

- In stations, the teacher or monitor may want to move, rather than moving the students.

- Keep in mind that simultaneous leads are a great reteaching or corrective opportunity. Groups don't always have to be mixed ability.

- Disruptive students often work better in a small, corrective group because of the adult's direct monitoring and personal feedback.

Lifesaver Tweaks

- For primary students, more monitoring may be needed at stations, and activities must be carefully planned to provide as much independence as possible.

- Parent volunteers work especially well at the elementary level.

- Secondary students might be able to take lead roles in facilitating station activities.

- Secondary students must see both partners as equally responsible for their grade and behavior management.

- All collaborative levels work for K–12 students.

Lifesaver Trip #1

http://www.nea.org/teachexperience/spedk031113.html

Dive into this site that focuses on six successful co-teaching strategies. Find your co-teaching style, strengths, and weaknesses before your collaboration voyage takes off.

Co-Planner

Classroom Teacher

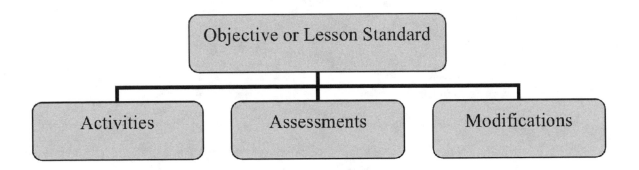

Media Specialist

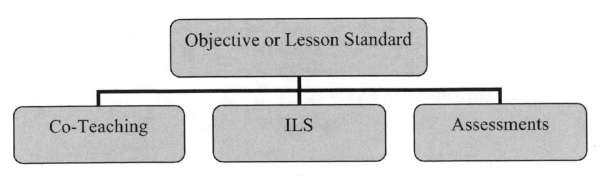

Note: ILS = Information Literacy Standards.

Lifesaver Tool #1

High-Five Collaboration Activities

When you dive into the waters of collaboration, you need to "sea" which activity will work best. The great thing is, you don't have to go into the water alone! Your partner is there every stroke of the way. The following five activities will get you—and your students—swimming toward your goals.

Jigsaw Groups

Your students won't be puzzled when they are highly engaged in active learning groups. Each group can have three to six members (fewer is sometimes better), with each team member responsible for a piece of the puzzle. As students become experts in the assigned area, they meet with other experts and prepare their teaching topic about what they are researching. Then the "experts" use resources provided by the teacher and media specialist to assist them in diving into the topic in greater depth. The groups then return to their original group to share what they have learned.

Community Circles

Community circles meet together after learning about the topic from the lead teacher. Heterogeneous groups meet to discuss and complete an activity to enhance their learning. Teams might participate in brainstorming, story mapping, predicting, and connecting (see Lifesaver Tools #2.1A, #2.1B, and # 2.2).

Super Sleuthing

Students are detectives in groups of two to six members. Each group works together to research and discover information on a given topic. Each group member has a preassigned role (see Lifesaver Trip #2). The final presentation may include an individual or group performance led by the new topic "investigators."

Research Retellers

Each member of an assigned group reads a different book on the same topic. After reading the texts, each member shares what he or she has learned with the small group, followed by the large group. Other members listen, provide feedback, and extend the learning based on their readings.

Substitute Teachers

Students work in groups to create quizzes or questions based on what they have read. The groups then collaborate and "test" their classmates.

Lifesaver Tips

- The planning time for the activities in this section is extensive but pays for itself during the implementation phase.

- Activities can also be used again with any lesson, saving valuable time later.

- Jigsaws work best with heterogeneous group members who can provide support to each other.

- Research and reading materials should be provided at a variety of reading levels and lexiles to ensure success for all students.

- Use a variety of texts and genres for all topics.

- Make sure computer resources are available during group work time.

Lifesaver Tweaks

- Enlist lots of help to implement the activities in this section at the primary level.

- Primary students may need to draw (in lieu of writing) and orally describe what they have learned.

- Secondary students need to be given options for when a group member is absent.

- At the primary level, "substitute teachers" would only work with a scribe (an older student or volunteer would work well).

- Explicit modeling should be done regardless of level.

Lifesaver Trip #2

http://litsite.alaska.edu/workbooks/circle/role.html

This site is perfect to help students dive into their new roles.

Name _____

Class _____

<u>Directions:</u> Write a summary of the story in the space below. In the bottom section, write your reflection of the story.

Summary:

_____
_____
_____
_____
_____
_____
_____
_____
_____
_____
_____

Reflection:

_____
_____
_____
_____
_____
_____
_____
_____
_____
_____
_____
_____
_____
_____
_____
_____

Lifesaver Tool #2.1A (Intermediate/Secondary)

Name _____

Date _____

<u>Directions:</u> Draw or write what the story was mostly about in the space below.

Summary:

My Review

I liked this book:

Yes :)   **No : (**   **So/So : /**

Why?

Lifesaver Tool #2.1B (Primary)

Name _____

Class _____ Date _____

<u>Directions:</u> Work with your group to complete the story map below.

Title _____

Author _____

1. Main Characters

2. Problems/Conflicts

3. Setting

4. Genre

5. Important Events/Plot

_____
_____
_____
_____
_____
_____
_____
_____

6. Resolution

Lifesaver Tool #2.2 (Intermediate/Secondary)

What Do You Need for Successful Collaboration?

Do you need to find out where to begin on your collaboration journey? This simple needs assessment can help you navigate your way through unfamiliar waters.

Using the needs assessment (see Lifesaver Tool #3) as a pre- and post-test can help you gather data on where you've been, where you are, and where you want to go. It is important to keep in mind that you are the only one who knows what is ultimately best for your students.

"Sea" What You Need

1. Have you determined which level of collaboration is best for your unit of study?

2. Have you adequately prepared your students for your collaborative activity?

3. Have you found time in your schedule to co-plan and collaborate?

4. Have you previewed all available resources?

5. Have you set reasonable goals with flexible time lines?

6. Have you reserved time available for resources (computer labs, media center, etc.)?

7. Have you purchased the additional resources to make this unit successful?

8. Have you reviewed information on successful co-teaching strategies?

9. Have you planned for unit evaluation and assessment?

10. Have you scheduled time for collaborative reflection at the completion of the unit?

Lifesaver Tips

• Provide the media specialist or teacher with information regarding specific modifications that may be needed for the students involved.

• Discuss the level of involvement needed with your collaborative partner.

• Be prepared to make schedule changes when more—or less—time is needed.

- Have a backup plan in the case of technology problems.

- Be honest in your communication with your collaborative partner. Provide reasonable and real suggestions for improvement.

- Arrange site visits for other collaborative schools in the area to "sea" the great things others are doing.

- Design a quantitative evaluation (a rubric works well) to gather collaborative unit data.

- Plan early . . . especially in cases when media staff is limited.

- Share your behavioral and academic expectations with your co-partner.

Lifesaver Tweaks

- Collaboration is easier with media specialists who have flexible schedules. Fixed schedules make planning time—and implementation—a challenge.

- Primary students may need frequent "brain breaks" during an especially challenging collaborative unit.

- Tweak your collaborative units by varying your instructional practices.

- Don't be afraid to tweak your collaborative unit midstream when necessary if things aren't going as well as expected.

- Use visual schedules to help students know the collaborative project time line (pictorial is great for primary, whereas a time line handout works well at the secondary level).

- Discuss each of your teaching and learning styles and be prepared to stretch and tweak those styles as needed.

Lifesaver Trip #3

http://www.tonibuzzeo.com/collaborativeunittemplate.pdf

Find a great collaborative unit template here! Surf's Up!

NEEDS ASSESSMENT FOR COLLABORATIVE UNIT
IMPLEMENTATION

Name_____   Date_____

Directions: The following prerequisites to implementation of effective collaborative unit models have been identified in the best-practice literature. Read each item carefully, reflect, and self-assess the need for professional development in your school for each area listed below. After completing this needs assessment, you will be more prepared to meet your individual professional development needs.

Preparation Needs Scale

    1 = below average

    2 = average

    3 = above average

    4 = strong

Do We Have a Clear and Common Vision?

1. _____ Collaborative partners have discussed their unit goals and objectives.

2. _____ Collaborative partners share a common vision, or have discussed the differences in vision.

3. _____ The school district is supportive and supports collaborative projects and a common vision.

4. _____ The school faculty is committed to co-teaching implementation.

5. _____ Key school personnel and administration have clear basic collaborative goals.

6. _____ Teachers are committed to building and maintaining professional relationships.

7. _____ Media specialist(s) are committed to building and maintaining professional relationships.

Lifesaver Tool #3

Are There Incentives for Implementation of Co-Teaching?

1. _____   Key players promoting co-teaching and collaboration are respected and trusted.

2. _____   The school and district are invested in the implementation of effective co-teaching models.

3. _____   Teachers have a vested interest in implementation of collaborative units.

4. _____   The school environment and culture promotes collaboration.

5. _____   Teachers are generally in favor of collaboration and co-teaching projects.

6. _____   Media specialist(s) are generally in favor of collaboration and co-teaching projects.

7. _____   The perception is that co-teaching benefits teachers.

8. _____   The perception is that co-teaching benefits students.

Do Key Personnel Possess Appropriate Background Knowledge and Skills?

1. _____   Administrators have participated in and support professional development for co-teaching and collaboration

2. _____   Teachers have actively participated in professional development opportunities for co-teaching and collaboration.

3. _____   Key personnel are committed to ongoing professional development for collaborative opportunities.

4. _____   Barriers to effective implementation of collaborative units arc recognized.

5. _____   There is open and positive communication between teachers and media specialist(s).

6. _____   The media specialist is able to deal with the diverse student population.

7. _____   Co-teaching is regularly occurring in our school.

8. _____   Co-teaching is successful in terms of student achievement.

9. _____   Co-teaching models provide a wider range of instructional opportunities than would be possible with just one teacher.

Lifesaver Tool #3

Literacy Lifesaver #4

Your "Standard" Collaborative Unit

As you plan your collaborative units, begin with a backward design starting with the standards. When you begin to plan, think about what you want your students to UNDERSTAND, KNOW, and be able to DO. Just as important, what standards will you meet as you achieve these goals and objectives? Lifesaver Tool #4 focuses on the American Association of School Librarian's Information Literacy Standards, but it's important to keep in mind that you will also be meeting critical subject-area standards (provided by the teacher). If that's not enough, you'll be meeting important technology and national reading standards as well. Perhaps collaborative units aren't all that standard after all—they're pretty "deep," aren't they?

Lifesaver Tips

- As you co-plan with your collaborative partner, provide him or her with a copy of the Information Literacy Standards (see Lifesaver Trip #61).

- Ask for a copy of the grade-level subject standards that you will meet.

- As you review the standards, you may see other areas of focus that your collaborative partner missed at first glance.

- Track the standards met on a checklist Lifesaver Tool #4. This type of data is extremely valuable in end-of-the-year reports and evaluation conferences with your administrators.

Lifesaver Tweaks

- Dive in with one or two standards and progress from there.

- At the elementary level, it is common to be meeting language arts standards while also meeting content-area standards.

- Be intentional with spiraling at all levels to ensure mastery.

- At the secondary level, provide the students with the posted standards that you are meeting in the collaborative unit.

Lifesaver Trip #4

http://www.lessonlocator.org/

This incredible site, designed for Indiana teachers, provides standards-based lesson plans for all grade and content levels. The user-friendly site is clickable and full of resources. Even if you're not a Hoosier, the lesson plans are fabulous, and standards are usually comparable from state to state. One of Tam's favorite diving-in links was the "Books Aligned to IN Standards" spot (K–8).

YOUR "STANDARD" CHECKLIST

Directions: Use the checklist below when you cover each content-area or library standard.

DATE	CLASS	UNIT	STANDARD	MASTERY

Lifesaver Tool #4

Partner Up: Are You a Good Collaborative Partner?

This lifesaver will help you decide whether you are (or are not) a good collaborative partner. Good collaborators are flexible, willing to change, and ready to try something new. Are you a risk-taker or reluctant to change? The three main reasons for resistance to change are as follows.

Self-Confidence:

- Can I really change?
- Can I really become a better teacher?

Skepticism:

- Students won't change, so why should I?
- Changing my teaching won't change poor student behavior, so why bother?

Status Quo:

- My students like me just the way I am, so why change?
- I get fine evaluations, why rock the boat?

Lifesaver Tips

1. Get to Know Your Partner.

   It is important to establish a good rapport with your co-teacher. It helps to know your partner on a personal level. What things do you have in common? Do you feel comfortable around the person? Establishing a good team rapport will help your students to feel more comfortable and make the climate more positive. (See Lifesaver Tool #5 for questions you can ask each other to get to know one another.)

2.   Discover Your Teaching Style . . . and Theirs!

It's great if your styles are similar—you'll work well together. However, different styles can add another dimension to your instruction. Either way, you're ready to set sail on your learning adventure.

3.   Can You Manage?

Knowing your managerial style will help you know how to work with your partner. If you know you are a control freak, for example, you can let your partner know your personality—and your expectations—up front. Discussing each other's strengths and weaknesses is a great, proactive way to ensure student and unit success.

4.   Discuss Your Students!

It can't be overstated how important it is to know the individual needs of the students you will be teaching. Each collaborative partner must know the personalities, behavior issues, and Individual Education Plans (IEPs) of students before the unit begins.

5.   Divide and Conquer

Decide up front how you will assess and who will grade or evaluate the finished project. Share the load and lighten the burden.

Lifesaver Tweaks

- You may sometimes need to tweak your own teaching style to meet your students' learning styles.

- You may also need to adjust your learning style to work effectively with your collaborative partner.

- No matter whether you are primary or secondary, choose the best collaboration level for when you find you are totally incompatible in style with your partner. It doesn't mean great learning can't take place. You just need to work around the weaknesses to find the strengths. Dividing and conquering may be best in this situation.

Lifesaver Trip #5

http://www.longleaf.net/teachingstyle.html

Find out your teaching style in a quick, online survey. This tool is a great conversation starter to use before you start your collaborative unit. You, and your partner, will be in style in no time!

Name _____ Date_____

"Who are you? Who? Who?
I really want to know!"

Answer the following questions as part of a getting-to-know-you activity. This could be done at a staff meeting for all teachers at the beginning of the year or individually for collaborative partners.

1. What is your favorite song or artist?

2. Tell me about your family.

3. What is your favorite season?

4. Do you collect anything?

5. What is your favorite childhood memory?

6. Are you a morning person or a night owl?

6. What is your favorite subject area to teach? Least favorite?

7. What would I be surprised to know about you?

Lifesaver Tool #5

Literacy Lifesaver #6

Blogging

Blogging is a great way to share the successes of your voyage. It's also a way to share concerns and frustrations, while getting helpful feedback from others through an interactive, Web-based discussion forum. One advantage of blogging is that you are able to keep a reflective journal throughout the process, while getting valuable insight from other crew members. Here are some different options to map out your course. Ahoy, mate!

Content-Related Blogging

Content-related blogging is a great way to get discussion started about a specific topic or course of study. It's a great tool to use with colleagues—or with students!

Instructional Blogging

This type of blogging is a way to share course announcements, deadlines, and critical information with your students.

Networking

Networking is a great way to discuss professional knowledge with others anywhere in the world. Education can be stressful, and it's nice to have a place to discuss that stress with others. If you've tried something that worked (or hasn't), this is a great place to share instructional strategies.

Lifesaver Tips

- Remember, unless it's a private blog, anyone can see it. Be professional in your postings.

- Never use student names in your blogging. Confidentiality of your students is key.

- New to blogging? Get online and join a blog already in process. When you're more experienced, start your own!

- Reviewing blogger profiles can help you find people who share your common interests or concerns.

- Post photos on your blog with caution. You'll need permission from parents to post pictures, even if you don't provide names.

- Lifesaver Tool #6 is a handy tool to post near your computer that lists these reminders.

Lifesaver Trip #6

http://www.blogger.com/tour_end.g

This blogging tool is absolutely free and includes support staff to help you on your blogging voyage. You can join a blog in-process, or start your own, with the click of a button. Custom colors and photo uploads can add creativity and personality. Happy blogging!

Blogging Tips for Beginners

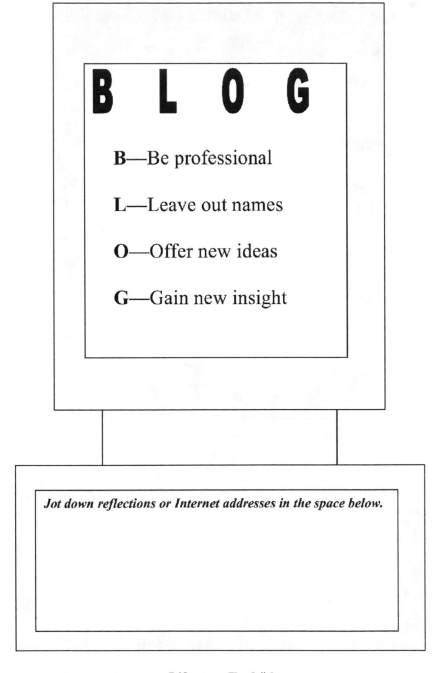

B L O G

B—Be professional

L—Leave out names

O—Offer new ideas

G—Gain new insight

Jot down reflections or Internet addresses in the space below.

Lifesaver Tool #6

Literacy Lifesaver #7

Carve Out Collaboration Time

Finding time to collaborate is one of the biggest hurdles and challenges educators face. While the motivation to implement great collaborative units may be there, time, sadly, may not be. Because there's no way to add time to the clock (you're already working long enough!), you must find ways to carve out time to chart your course and navigate through collaborative waters. Lifesaver Tool #7 provides a planning sheet to use with your co-teachers.

Lifesaver Tips

- Community Collaboration Days

    Invite a guest speaker in to share information with students that fits a specific unit or standard. The time that the speaker is presenting is a great opportunity for partners to touch base informally and get the ball rolling. Teams can share release time for planning. Parent volunteers may also be used to monitor students while teachers and media specialists meet for collaboration discussions.

- Common Planning Time

    Ideally, the administrator assists with carving out collaboration time by providing common planning time during preparation periods, lunches, or after-school meetings.

- Principal Planning Time

    If the principal is supportive, he or she can provide opportunities for collaboration. For example, teachers could co-plan during a scheduled convocation at the elementary level. At the secondary level, planning could occur during an event-specific time, such as a pep rally, counseling corner, or homeroom.

- Lunch Bunch

    The most common planning time might occur during lunch. If arranged in advance, the media specialist can lunch with teachers by using a parent volunteer or assistant to cover or using blocked out time on a flexible schedule.

- Double Up

  If you have the opportunity to double up a class with a partner teacher, planning time with the media specialist can occur.

- Compute Some Planning Time

  When students are working independently in the computer lab, the teacher and media specialist could steal a few minutes for some much-needed collaborative moments.

Lifesaver Tweaks

- At the elementary level, collaboration opportunities could be found during a time when "specials" (PE, music, art, library) are taking place. If the special is library, this is a perfect opportunity to co-plan. If planned in advance, the media specialist can plan independent work time for students so that much-needed planning time can occur naturally.

- Utilizing student teachers or university students can be a valuable resource to provide planning time.

- Beware, primary teachers! It is important that students be working in the computer lab on something that has been previously taught or modeled on which they have total independence.

- Beware, secondary teachers! It is critical that students be provided with a standards-based, engaging activity that they can work on independently. You don't want to be constantly interrupted during valuable planning time to remind students to get off music video sites or e-mail!

- The media specialist may be able to come into the classroom while students are working independently at stations or during sustained silent reading time. This is also a great time for the media specialist to do observational assessment of students prior to the collaborative unit.

Lifesaver Trip #7

http://www.teachingexpertise.com/articles/declutter-save-time-232

This site includes much-needed information on saving time and simplifying your life. Who doesn't need a few ideas for "smooth sailing"?

DIVE IN!

(Collaborative Planning Sheet)

Date: _____ Teacher:_____ Grade:_____

Please list units/standards you would be interested in collaborating on this month.

Language Arts **(Author Studies/Book Titles)**

Science

Social Studies

Health

Math

Other

Lifesaver Tool #7

Literacy Lifesaver #8

Collaboration Conditions

Whether you sink or swim during your collaborative unit depends on a number of different factors. Some of the factors you can control (yippee!); others can't be controlled (boo!). With the factors over which you have no control, you must work collaboratively not only with other teachers but with administrators and leadership teams to create a shared vision of supportive learning communities.

Lifesaver Tips

- Work to support a sense of collaborative community.

- Meet with your principal or administrator to share your concerns openly regarding your school's collaborative climate. Lifesaver Tool #8 (Collaboration: Smooth Sailing or Choppy Waters?) can provide progress data to share at this meeting.

- Be positive when movements toward a shared vision occur. Don't let negativity discourage you from moving forward. Change is messy, but worthwhile.

- Stay focused on the goal of student achievement.

- Keep physical barriers in mind. How can you break down the physical barriers to keep them from preventing collaborative projects? For example, how can you build better rapport with a teacher in the farthest part of the building? How can you build rapport with a teacher who travels between schools (this could very well be the media specialist)?

- Investigate the abundance of collaborative resources available.

- Blogging is a great way to find out about hot new resources.

- Continue to strive toward building trust and respect among colleagues in your building (it's easier with some than others)!

Lifesaver Tweaks

The tips in this section are appropriate for all K–12 teachers and media specialists. If you are in a school that has not studied or been involved in learning communities and gone through that process, the learning curve or time needed for the implementation of collaborative learning may need to be tweaked.

Lifesaver Trip #8

http://www.tonibuzzeo.com/bookscollaboration.html

Get all the buzz on collaboration here. This site features resources by outstanding teacher-librarian-author Toni Buzzeo. An online collaborative planning form is also just a click away!

Collaboration: Smooth Sailing or Choppy Waters?

Rate using the following key:

+   (Positive change observed)

–   (Negative change observed)

NC (No change observed)

Teacher Results:

- Teachers are no longer as isolated because of collaboration projects.

- There is an increased effort to meet the shared vision of the school.

- There is more shared responsibility for students' success.

- Teachers are trying new collaborative strategies.

- Teacher climate and rapport has improved because of professional development and collaboration.

- Teacher absenteeism has improved.

- There is a greater amount of risk-taking and commitment to lasting change.

- Teachers communicate to solve problems and reduce conflicts.

Student Results:

- Fewer absent students.

- Fewer tardy students.

- Increased student achievement.

- Improved grades and project completion.

- Reduced achievement gaps among students.

- Greater respect for diversity of students shown.

Lifesaver Tool #8

Literacy Lifesaver #9

Rubric Ratings

OK, you've met together and planned and planned and planned. Now what? It's time to find out what your students have gained as a result of all of your collaborative efforts. Gathering student feedback in terms of student surveys is helpful, but even more helpful is the quantitative data you've collected at the unit's end. Rubrics are the best—and easiest—way to gather quantitative data (see Lifesaver Tool #9 for an example). A good rubric can provide valuable feedback to you, the teacher/media specialist, the parents, and, perhaps most important, the student. Following are some benefits of using rubrics for student assessment.

Lifesaver Tips

- Rubrics are helpful tools for assessing information that can be somewhat subjective.

- Rubrics communicate expectations up front (no surprises later) with students (and your collaborative partner).

- Rubrics can also provide valuable information to parents (unfortunately for students, in some cases).

- Rubrics provide immediate feedback on a student's strengths and weaknesses and can be used to evaluate growth or progress over time.

- Rubrics are great tools to share during grade-level collaboration meetings.

Lifesaver Tweaks

- Although rubrics are appropriate for all K–12 students, they can easily be tweaked to meet the needs of a new lesson, grade level, or class (see Lifesaver Trip #9).

- You may want to assign points to various rubric categories for quantitative data collection (also known as grades!).

- At the primary level, rubrics can include pictures with words (such as a "hamburger rubric").

- At the secondary level, rubrics can (and should) be developed with the students.

Lifesaver Trip #9

http://www.rcampus.com/

This amazing site allows you to create your rubrics or search through thousands of rubrics already created and ready to use with the click of a mouse. Although you have to be a member to access all of the services (including a blog site and collaboration page), membership is free. After you surf to this site, you won't have to navigate anywhere else—it's all smooth sailing from here!

Name_____

Class_____

Date_____

Rubric for Student Projects

Objective/Standard	Needs Improvement 1	In Progress 2	Mastery 3

Lifesaver Tool #9

Literacy Lifesaver #10

Did You Make the Grade? Evaluating Collaboration

Now that you know all there is to know about collaboration, it's time to give yourself a score on the success of your collaborative project. It is important for you—and your partner—to take time to reflect on the successes and challenges of the unit before setting sail on other projects. The sharing of ideas and discussion over effective (and ineffective, in some cases) techniques can be rewarding for both of you. When you get ready to meet at the unit's end, discuss the following questions:

1. Was the level of collaboration appropriate for what you intended?

2. What teaching strategies were the most and least effective?

3. What alternate strategies might you try next time?

4. Were the majority of students successful in meeting unit standards or objectives?

5. What modifications would you make for students?

6. What might you do exactly the same?

7. What might you do differently the next time you implement the unit?

8. Was your monitoring of student progress successful?

9. Did both you and your partner share in the planning, implementation, and evaluation of the unit?

10. Did you measure the effectiveness in terms of student achievement?

Lifesaver Tips

- To save time, consider providing your co-partner with a hard copy of the preceding reflective questions prior to meeting.

- An e-mail or discussion blog can be a valuable way to communicate if schedules don't allow face-to-face time.

- As far as reflection and evaluation go, the sooner they take place, the better. If you wait too long, time will get away from you, and you'll have forgotten valuable key points.

- At the end of the unit, request materials now for next year's unit. It's never too soon to start gathering resource materials.

Lifesaver Tweaks

- Use student surveys to reflect on your unit and help guide your answers to the preceding questions.

- See Lifesaver Tool #10 for a unit evaluation.

Lifesaver Trip #10

http://teacher.scholastic.com/tools/todo.htm

Scholastic.com is an awesome site for thousands of quality resources. This link is no exception. The online Teacher To-Do List is a great forum to record to-do's and reminders during your collaborative project. The evaluation coast will be clear when you go to answer your critical questions.

Collaborative Unit Evaluation

Teacher/Grade/Department_____

Collaborative Unit of Study_____

. . . .

Strengths: What do you think went well?

. . . .

Suggestions: What could be improved?

. . . .

What resources were the most beneficial?

. . . .

How well did the level of collaboration help to meet the unit objectives or standards?

. . . .

Other comments:

. . . .

Time allotment:

    Cooperative planning _____
    Actual teaching time _____

Lifesaver Tool #10

Lifesaver Notes

_____
_____
_____
_____
_____
_____
_____
_____
_____
_____
_____
_____
_____
_____
_____
_____
_____
_____
_____
_____
_____

Lifesaver Notes

_____

_____

_____

_____

_____

_____

_____

_____

_____

_____

_____

_____

_____

_____

_____

_____

_____

_____

_____

_____

_____

Chapter 2

Utilizing Different Genres

Literacy Lifesaver #11

Dive into Different Genres

A perfect opportunity for collaboration between the library media specialist and classroom teacher can be found in genre research. Often, teachers and students find themselves focusing on one (or their favorite) genre. This lifesaver unit will get their feet wet as they wade into different types of reading. While researching different genres, students have the option to explore writers' crafts in different, perhaps previously uncharted, territories. When students are exposed to different genres in their readings, they will be more successful when they write in different genres and formats.

The media specialist's role in genre research is critical. Whether teachers utilize nursery rhymes at literacy stations ("Rhyme Times") or just through independent research, they will depend heavily on the media specialist to support them on this trip out to "sea" what genres are available. The media specialist will need to provide annotated biographies, pull available books, research different versions, search for appropriate Internet links, and act as a "second mate" on board.

Following is an outline of the different genres we will navigate in our quest to motivate students to read a wider variety of books. Each genre has its own purpose, format, and unique characteristics.

Lifesaver Tips

- Nursery Rhymes
- Tall Tales, Folktales, and Fairy Tales
- Mysteries
- Picture Books
- Biographies
- Poetry/Verse Novels
- Plays

- NonFiction/Informational Books

- Fiction Novels (Historical, Realistic, Fantasy, Science Fiction)

Lifesaver Tweaks

The order in which the teacher and media specialist present the genres should be based on the developmental and interest levels of their student group. Often, students will become highly motivated when they see the excitement of teachers. Linking the books to a purpose is also a way to increase involvement and student engagement. Thematic connections provide a built-in purpose and help students link critical background knowledge while studying different genres. Use Lifesaver Tool #11 to provide students a format for reporting on their selected genre studies. Note: Primary students may need to respond orally to the review sheet, whereas secondary students can complete the form individually or in small, cooperative groups.

Lifesaver Trip #11

http://www.readwritethink.org/lesson_images/lesson270/genre_books.pdf

This site provides a nice list of quality literature characterized by different genres. While the focus is on intermediate and older students, some primary books are included. In addition, many titles could be used as interactive read-alouds at the primary level.

Genre Group Book Review

General Information

Name _____

Title _____

Author _____

Genre _____

Total number of pages _____

CHARACTERS—List the main characters and describe them.

SETTING—When and where does the story take place?

PLOT—List the main problem(s) and solution(s).

PERSONAL OPINION—What rating do you give this book?

List your reasons *why*.

Loved it!

Liked it.

Okay.

Not my favorite.

Hated it!

Lifesaver Tool #11

From *100+ Literacy Lifesavers: A Survival Guide for Librarians and Teachers K–12* by Pamela S. Bacon and Tammy K. Bacon. Westport, CT: Libraries Unlimited. Copyright © 2009.

Literacy Lifesaver #12

Rhyme Time

Nursery rhymes are loved by readers young and old. The charm, rhythm, and familiar stories (like wrapping yourself in your grandmother's sweater) make this genre irresistible. Too often, young children come to school without ever having heard them. Repeating nursery rhymes is a buried treasure that needs to be discovered. Even for older students, comparing and contrasting the different versions can be a powerful learning voyage. Older students can also practice valuable fluency skills by reading aloud nursery rhymes to younger students.

Lifesaver Tips

- Explicitly teach key elements, including rhyme schemes and story sequence.

- Primary children can sing nursery rhymes as they begin to develop print concepts.

- Teachers and media specialists should recite nursery rhymes while using the text for shared reading.

- Singing nursery rhymes can help younger students learn to read.

- Acting out rhymes helps students learn sequencing skills.

- Nursery rhymes provide an excellent way to build phonemic awareness.

- Laminate teacher-created nursery rhyme charts to hang on pants hangers at chart stands that are within easy reach for students and that they can easily carry to their work stations for rereading.

- Use sentence strips with nursery rhymes for sequencing practice on a pocket chart as a managed independent learning-station activity.

- Use highlighters with elementary students to find rhyming words after many opportunities for shared reading.

- Cutting out highlighted words (from the previous tip) and pasting them on classroom charts is a great extension activity.

- Create new endings for nursery rhymes (Humpty Dumpty needs help!).

- Have students create character puppets and act out the rhyme at a drama station.

- Post visual organizers for primary students for independent work at the "Rhyme Time" station (see Lifesaver Tool #12.1).

- Have students interview parents and grandparents to find out which nursery rhymes they were told. Chart the results together in class.

- See the Nursery Rhyme Pre-Test in Lifesaver Tool #12.2.

Lifesaver Tweaks

- Tie in nursery rhymes with thematic connections. For example, "Ring around the Rosy" was actually written at the time of the Black Death, or the Plague, when the bubonic plague wiped out a huge percent of Europe's population.

- Have struggling readers create a rap that extends a nursery rhyme.

- Older students might enjoy videotaping themselves acting out the nursery rhyme and presenting it to younger students.

- Older students can also create their own PowerPoint presentations of nursery rhymes.

- Involve the media specialist when creating PowerPoint presentations with students (You'll need extra help—all hands on deck!).

- Have students research the background of famous nursery rhymes to see where they originated.

- Don't assume older students have background knowledge of nursery rhymes. Sadly, some students don't know them at all.

- Work with the media specialist to have older students rotate among nursery rhymes. For secondary students, include information about the times in which the rhymes were written (history).

Lifesaver Trips #12

http://curry.edschool.virginia.edu/go/wil/rimes_and_rhymes.htm

Find a nursery rhyme for each week for early literacy instruction. Dive in!

http://www.hubbardscupboard.org/kindergarten_rhyme_time.html

Here's a wealth of resources for nursery rhyme activities that throw out the parent involvement lifeline.

http://www.bbc.co.uk/dna/h2g2/A288966

Use this site for a great research starting point for older students. Several rhymes are included with background information—it's fascinating!

RHYME TIME STATION

1. READ 📖

2. PUT IT TOGETHER 📁

3. REREAD 📖

4. DRAW ✍

5. WRITE ✏

Lifesaver Tool #12.1

Nursery Rhyme Pre-Test

1. What nursery rhyme states, "The cow jumped over the moon"?

2. Who lived in a cupboard?

3. What is the line that follows "Twinkle, twinkle, little star"?

4. Why did Jack and Jill run up the hill?

5. What nursery rhyme asks the question, "Have You Any Wool?"

Literacy Lifesaver #12.2

Answers to Nursery Rhyme Pre-Test (Literacy Lifesaver #12.2)

1. "Hey Diddle Diddle"
2. Old Mother Hubbard
3. "How I wonder what you are."
4. To fetch a pail of water.
5. "Baa Baa Black Sheep"

Tell-Tale Starts

Who doesn't like to hear a great tall tale or a fractured fairy tale read aloud? Believe it or not, like traditional nursery rhymes, many students come to us without critical background knowledge surrounding this genre. Again, the media specialist's role is critical in uncovering the latest versions, ordering them or borrowing them (sometimes from across the street; other times from across the state) to have ready when the time comes. This is also an excellent opportunity for the media specialist to schedule guest readers to "tale" their favorite story.

Lifesaver Tips

- Explicitly teach the key elements of each of the folktales: Setting, Main Character(s), Problem, and Solution (see Lifesaver Tool #13.1).

- Include the students in creating the assessment rubric for this chapter (see Lifesaver Tool #13.2).

- Explore the unique elements found in folktales and fairy tales (students can refer to Lifesaver Tool #13.3 posted in the classroom for easy reference).

- Compare and contrast different versions using Venn diagrams.

- Use Kidspiration/Inspiration software program to design custom-made story maps of tales.

Lifesaver Tweaks

- Provide rich opportunities for students to act out their favorite tales or create products involving modified versions (great for kinesthetic learners).

- Enrich the skills of visual learners by having them draw the tale using a storyboard format.

- Enrich the skills of musical/rhythmic students by having them create a song or rap to extend their learning.

- Older students can write reviews of tall tales. Invite the media specialist in to demonstrate how he or she uses reviews to purchase specific books.

- Make customized book jackets for "special" classroom or media center books.

- Make "Student Recommends" signs and ask the media center to post the signs around the media center.

Lifesaver Trip #13

http://www.educationworld.com/a_tech/tech/tech066.shtml

No matter if you're a techie or a newbie, this site allows you (and your students) a chance to participate in a Fairy Tale and Folk Tale Cyber Dictionary project. Even better, the project can be enjoyed by all with easy and suggested adaptations.

Name_____ Date_____

Tell-Tale Parts

Folktale Title: _____ Author: _____

Setting (Where and when does the folktale take place?)

_____

_____

_____

_____

Main Character (Who is the folktale mostly about?)

_____

_____

_____

_____

Problem (What is the main problem in the folktale?)

_____

_____

_____

_____

Solution (How was the problem solved?)

_____

_____

_____

_____

Lifesaver Tool #13.1

Tell-Tale Parts: Writing Rubric

Name(s): _____

Tall Tale Title: _____

Date: _____

After writing original tall tales (individually or with a partner), students will provide proof from their story that relates to key elements of a tall tale. Comments about the students' writing can be recorded below.

Tall Tale Elements	Proof	Comments
Story is very exaggerated.		
Main character(s) has a conflict/problem to solve.		
Main character shows super-human strength.		
Plot is humorous and impossible, with lots of action.		
The main character solves a problem/conflict, overcomes an obstacle, or defeats the "bad guy" (antagonist).		

Lifesaver Tool #13.2

From *100+ Literacy Lifesavers: A Survival Guide for Librarians and Teachers K–12* by Pamela S. Bacon and Tammy K. Bacon. Westport, CT: Libraries Unlimited. Copyright © 2009.

Tall Tales Tips

- Tall tales are usually set in the past.

- Be creative! Include make-believe aspects.

- Include clearly defined character traits.

- Tall tales may include people, events, or objects.

- Choose a plot that includes a problem or conflict that needs to be solved.

- Usually tall tales have happy endings, based on the resolution of the conflict or problem.

- Often a tall tale teaches a lesson or demonstrates important values.

Lifesaver Tool #13.3

Searching for Great Literacy Is No Mystery!

It's no mystery that the Internet is becoming the most powerful lesson-planning resource for teachers and media specialists. With the click of a mouse, a lesson plan that used to take hours to create now literally takes seconds. Although there is no way even to touch the surface of all that is available, your media specialist can help you narrow down and select resources that are just right for your needs. In this chapter, we are highlighting some of our favorite resources so that great ideas are no longer a mystery for busy professionals!

Lifesaver Tips

- Explicitly teach the key elements of a mystery: a puzzle or problem to solve (often involving a crime situation), clues, suspects, motives, and a solution. (Lifesaver Tool #14.1 gives readers a chance to record these four key elements.)

- Bring in a briefcase and pull out items to represent clues in a mystery that you are getting ready to read for a great anticipatory set.

- Use mysteries to engage reluctant students in both reading and writing activities.

- Choose mysteries that will motivate reluctant readers.

- Include a variety of questions from Bloom's Taxonomy, which easily lends itself to this genre.

- Use the think-aloud strategy to help students solve mysteries. It takes practice!

- Allow students to talk through their clues together to solve mysteries (use the "Say Something" strategy with knee-to-knee partners at the primary level or with Kagan cooperative learning groups at the upper levels). "Sea" the glossary for further information about these cooperative strategies.

- Model the reader's notebook process using a large chart turned sideways so that students can complete this activity independently as they read more chapters. It is helpful if the media specialist or assistant can act as a scribe.

- Choose activities to meet all learning styles.

- Discover the writing ability of older students as they write their own mysteries.

Lifesaver Tweaks

- Use interactive read-alouds to introduce primary students to this genre while providing high levels of support.

- Assist younger students in writing their own mysteries as a shared writing or interactive writing activity.

- Dive into mysteries with secondary students by using "The Haunted House Mystery" video kit. To order this video, go to http://www.hrmvideo.com.

- Lifesaver Tool #14.2 gives students in cooperative groups a chance to see "whodunit."

Lifesaver Trips #14

http://www.readwritethink.org/lessons/lesson_view.asp?id=796

This site includes extensive lesson plans for a variety of mystery genre activities. Go search! (We're glad this site is no longer a mystery!)

http://www.readwritethink.org/materials/mystery_cube/

Use this great online activity at the primary level to complete together with shared writing on a presentation screen about a common book. At the intermediate and secondary levels, this activity can be done independently or in cooperative groups. See what I mean, Sherlock?

http://www.teacher.scholastic.com/writewit/mystery/

Discover this interactive mystery writing activity featuring author Joan Lowery Nixon. It's so good, it's scary!

http://content.scholastic.com/browse/lessonplan.jsp?id=660

Introduce students to the mystery genre and give them the opportunity to act like real detectives and solve mysteries. Everything you need to implement this mystery unit is here for you!

Lifesaver Tool #14.1

The Haunted House Mystery

After careful and thoughtful deliberation, we _____ (insert group name) have decided that the following person(s) is guilty of haunting the Peabody House:

_____

_____

_____

_____

_____

_____

_____

_____

As a result, we believe the following sentence should be served…

We base our decisions on the following facts:

1.

2.

3.

Lifesaver Tool #14.2

Picture This!

They say a picture is worth a thousand words. In this case, a picture book is worth a thousand resources. Clearly, picture books are great tools to use with students of all ages. By reading aloud to young children, you allow them to access concepts and vocabulary that they could not read independently. Older students, however, still benefit from picture books as they practice key concepts and participate in visualization activities. Picture books can level the playing field for all readers by creating experiences that build rich background knowledge through text. Because of the media specialist's expertise with new books, recommended books, and award-winning books, he or she should be called on to assist with developing, planning, implementing, and evaluating your picture-book unit.

Lifesaver Tips

- Expose students to a variety of picture books in your classroom (experts suggest three to six read-alouds per day—perfect opportunities for picture books).

- Include an array of picture books. Be sure to include both fiction and nonfiction (informational) picture books.

- Utilize read-alouds as a powerful comprehension strategy with your students (see Lifesaver Tool #15).

- Provide students with the opportunity to hear the voices of both the media specialist and the classroom teacher with fluent, expressive reading.

- Read picture books with your students to practice "noticing" both oral and visual examples of an author's language and voice. This practice allows students to "stand on the author's shoulders" when they begin writing their own books.

- Utilize sticky notes for planning to highlight key vocabulary and concepts you don't want to overlook. Encourage older students to do the same by modeling the procedure. Revisit the same picture book often to provide students with a chance to dive deeper into the book with retelling, summarizing, and recalling main ideas.

- Compare and contrast popular picture books using Venn diagrams.

- Stop reading at key points to model and allow students to practice making predictions.

- Use wordless picture books with students for great writing prompts (scribe for primary students).

Lifesaver Tweaks

- Picture books are now being created with older students in mind. Don't hesitate to use this strategy.

- Writing and illustrating alternative endings to fairy tales is a great extension activity for older students—writing and illustrating their own is even better!

- Use picture books with older students to teach key concepts and themes without getting bogged down in deeper texts.

- Teach key science and social studies standards through picture books.

Lifesaver Trips #15

http://pd-network.com/lessons/partner_think_alouds.pdf

At this site, literacy expert Linda Hoyt shares partner think-aloud strategies in an easy-to-follow, step-by-step strategy. Hoyt's *Interactive Read-Alouds* (2006) books are standards-focused print tools you won't want to miss.

http://www.carolhurst.com/subjects/criticalpicture.html

Hurst's site focuses on excellent step-by-step lessons to help older students look critically at fairy tales. You—and your students—will get the picture in no time!

Read-Aloud Tips

R—Read for fun!

E—Enjoy it!

A—Act out favorite parts.

D—Demonstrate expressive language.

A—Always plan ahead and practice.

L—Listen to student responses and predictions.

O—Offer your insight and connections.

U—Utilize different questioning strategies.

D—Do a picture walk.

S—Show pictures and writer's craft clearly.

Lifesaver Tool #15

Literacy Lifesaver #16

What's Up, People?

Biographies are a great way to learn about people, past and present. Older students especially enjoy researching famous people—usually famous athletes and movie stars. It is important that students understand that history can come alive by reading the biographies of famous people, not just by watching movies, such as *Night at the Museum* (an excellent movie tie-in for this unit, however!).

Lifesaver Tips

- Explicitly teach key elements of a biography.

- Write bio-poems to reinforce key concepts (see instructions and an example at http://www.readwritethink.org/lesson_images/lesson398/biopoem.pdf).

- Assist students with selecting a biography about a person who interests them and will keep them highly motivated.

- Utilize the media specialist to help you gather a variety of high-interest biographies (some may need to be borrowed from your local public library).

- Refer the media specialist to Lifesaver Tool #16.1 for a variety of high-interest biographies for possible purchasing.

- Use time lines (see Lifesaver Tool #16.3) to help students gain perspectives of different time periods.

- Use K-W-L charts for this genre (K = What I **K**now; W = What I **W**ant to Know; L = What I **L**earned).

- Use literature circles to provide students with free choice and enriched discussion groups during the biography unit.

Lifesaver Tweaks

- Have primary students create life-size outlines of their bodies and decorate them with outfits that represent their ancestry or other important characteristics. Students may then prepare an oral report to present to family members or other classrooms (modified gallery walk). Lifesaver Tool #16.2 is a short feedback form to use during the presentations.

- Read aloud picture-book biographies regularly at the primary level.

- Use author studies to help primary students connect with the lives of authors through a biography study.

- Model picture walks with a biography to help younger students gain key understandings.

- Have primary students decorate paper lunch sacks to represent the subject of their chosen biography. Place three items (for younger students) inside the bag to represent their learning. Older students can write key facts on index cards to extend their learning.

Lifesaver Trips #16

http://www.fno.org/bio/biomak2.htm

The "Biography Maker" site helps younger students navigate through the writing of their own biographies.

http://readwritethink.org/materials/bio_cube/

The "Bio Cube" is a great lesson to use with students as they independently read their biographies.

Biographies and Memoirs

This document is reprinted with permission from **Carol Hurst's Children's Literature Site** at http://www.carolhurst.com. Copyright © 1996–2008, Rebecca Otis.

Bruchac, Joseph. **Crazy Horse's Vision.** Illustrator: S. D. Nelson
Lee & Low, 2000. ISBN 1880000946.
Rating: 4 Stars
Grades: 2–6
> The stylized illustrations help to tell the story of the years of the great chief's childhood up until he got his name, which was "Crazy Horse" in English or "Tashunka Witco" in Lakota.

Byars, Betsy. **The Moon & I**
Beech Tree, 1996. ISBN 0688137040.
Rating: 4 Stars
Grades: 3–9
> With a light and humorous touch, Ms. Byars tells of her life, her passions, and the way that she writes her books.

Carle, Eric. **The Art of Eric Carle**
Philomel, 1996. ISBN 039922937X.
Rating: 4 Stars
Grades: 1–9
> This is a wonderful source book for information about the picture-book author and his work.

Carlson, Laurie. **Boss of the Plains: The Hat That Won the West.** Illustrator: Holly Meade
DK Publishing, 1998. ISBN 0613284275.
Rating: 3 Stars
Grades: K–2
> John Batterson Stetson didn't find much gold in the rush to California, but the hat maker from New Jersey did invent the wide-brimmed hat that was to become a symbol of the west.

Cleary, Beverly. **A Girl from Yamhill: A Memoir**
Bantam, 1989. ISBN 0380727404.
Rating: 2 Stars
Grades: 5–9
> This is Beverly Cleary's own story from birth to her departure for college. Her first few years were spent on a farm isolated even from the small town of Yamhill. Her mother's overbearing and strict nature further isolated Beverly. Eventually her parents quit farming and moved the family to Portland, where her father worked as a night watchman and Beverly entered

public school, which, at first, was a disaster, much to her mother's embarrassment. Later Beverly made friends and succeeded academically.

Cleary, Beverly. **My Own Two Feet**
Morrow, 1995. ISBN 0380727463.
Rating: 3 Stars
Grades: 5–9

This book takes up where *A Girl from Yamhill* left off with Beverly's departure for college. Leaving home didn't mean the end of problems with her mother and, as in the first volume, Cleary makes no attempt to slide over that relationship. During college, she lived with her aunt, and the incidents of her college life and romances are remembered clearly. The book offers a good perspective on growing up in the 1930s.

Cooney, Barbara. **Eleanor**
Viking, 1999. ISBN 0670861596.
Rating: 3 Stars
Grades: 3–9

This is an insightful rendition of the painful childhood years of Eleanor Roosevelt, whose emancipation came during her boarding school years in London.

Dahl, Roald. **Boy: Tales of Childhood**
Puffin, 2001. ISBN 0141303050.
Rating: 3 Stars
Grades: 5–9

In many ways, this is a bitter account of the bullies and authority figures who were a large part of Dahl's childhood. Among the bitterness, however, is hilarity as we witness the rebellious young boy dealing with his oppressors.

Dash, Joan. **The Longitude Prize.** Illustrator: Dusan Petricic
Francis Foster Books, 2000. ISBN 0374346364.
Rating: 3 Stars
Grades: 5–9

In a handsome book with wonderfully light illustrations, Dash tells the complex story of an invention by an equally complex man, clock maker John Harrison, who invented the device to measure longitude.

Demi. **The Dalai Lama**
Holt, 1998. ISBN 080505443X.
Rating: 3 Stars
Grades: 2–8

This beautifully illustrated picture book contains some of the Buddhist beliefs and the Dalai's efforts toward peace.

Frank, Anne. **Anne Frank: The Diary of a Young Girl**

Prentice Hall, 1992. ISBN 0553296981.

Rating: 4 Stars

Grades: 6–9

> The diary has been the basis of both a play and a movie. It is important for the account it gives us of the persecution of the Jews, but even more important for the intimate portrait of the hopeful young girl.

Freedman, Russell. **Eleanor Roosevelt: A Life of Discovery**

Clarion, 1993. ISBN 0899198627.

Rating: 4 Stars

Grades: 5–9

> Freedman's biography of one of the most influential and controversial first ladies of America creates the full-bodied picture of the activist who served as her husband's legs—and often his conscience.

Freedman, Russell. **Franklin Delano Roosevelt**

Clarion, 1990. ISBN 0395629780.

Rating: 4 Stars

Grades: 5–9

> Freedman makes the life of the charismatic leader vivid and engaging for all readers, using photographs liberally.

Freedman, Russell. **Lincoln: A Photobiography**

Clarion, 1989. ISBN 0899193803.

Rating: 4 Stars

Grades: 4–9

> Freedman received the Newbery Award for this masterful biography of Lincoln in which the complicated nature of the witty storyteller and astute politician, who was at times overwhelmed by melancholy, is revealed.

Fritz, Jean. **And Then What Happened, Paul Revere?** Illustrator: Margaret Tomes

Putnam, 1996. ISBN 0698113519.

Rating: 3 Stars

Grades: 2–6

> This was the first of Jean Fritz's short biographies of Revolutionary War heroes. She fills in the portrait of Paul Revere and his times in a light but factual manner.

Fritz, Jean. **Bully for You, Teddy Roosevelt**

Putnam, 1997. ISBN 039921769X.

Rating: 3 Stars

Grades: 4–8

> In one of her longer biographies, Fritz tells the story of the frail child who became a zestful, enthusiastic, and charismatic leader.

Fritz, Jean. **Can't You Make Them Behave, King George?** Illustrator: Tomie dePaola
Putnam, 1996. ISBN 0698114027.

Rating: 4 Stars

Grades: 2–8

Fritz's portrait of King George III is fascinating as we see the American Revolution from the British—or at least the king's—point of view.

Fritz, Jean. **The Great Little Madison**
Putnam, 1998. ISBN 0399217681.

Rating: 3 Stars

Grades: 5–9

In this book, we begin to understand the personality of this little man, as well as his effect on United States history.

Fritz, Jean. **Leonardo's Horse.** Illustrator: Hudson Talbott
Putnam, 2001. ISBN 0399235760.

Rating: 3 Stars

Grades: 3–9

First conceived by Leonardo da Vinci, the huge statue of a horse was to stand in front of a duke's palace in Italy. This is the biography of a statue that was started by da Vinci and finished centuries later.

Fritz, Jean. **Traitor: The Case of Benedict Arnold**
Puffin, 1981. ISBN 0140329404.

Rating: 4 Stars

Grades: 4–9

As always, with Jean Fritz's work, the book is carefully researched, and she invents and assumes nothing. Read about Arnold's heroism in earlier times, his later greed, and, at last, his incredible treachery.

Fritz, Jean. **What's the Big Idea, Ben Franklin?** Illustrator: Margot Tomes
Scott Foresman, 1996. ISBN 0698113721.

Rating: 3 Stars

Grades: 2–6

Fritz's light shines brightly on the engaging and eccentric inventor who became so influential in the American political and scientific world.

Fritz, Jean. **Why Don't You Get a Horse, Sam Adams?** Illustrator: Trina Schart Hyman
Putnam, 1999. ISBN 0808544853.

Rating: 3 Stars

Grades: 2–8

This is the eccentric man who became a leader of the Revolution and strode about Boston because he refused to ride a horse.

Fritz, Jean. **Will You Sign Here, John Hancock?** Illustrator: Trina Schart Hyman
Paper Star, 1997. ISBN 069811440X.
Rating: 4 Stars
Grades: 2–6

      The wealthy, rather foppish man, who became one of the mainstays and financiers of the American Revolution, is given a light coverage in this brief bicentennial biography.

Hopkins, Lee Bennett. **Been to Yesterdays: Poem of a Life**
Boyds Mills, 1995. ISBN 1563974673.
Rating: 4 Stars
Grades: 5–9

      Twenty-nine separate poems combine to tell a story of the disintegration of the author's family.

Houston, Jeanne Wakatsuki. **Farewell to Manzanar**
Houghton Mifflin, 2002. ISBN 0618216200.
Rating: 4 Stars
Grades: 4–9

      One of the first families to be relocated to a Japanese internment camp in the California mountains was the Wakatsuki family, who were forced to abandon a thriving fishing business in Long Beach and take only what they could carry.

Hurst, Carol Otis. **Rocks in His Head** Illustrator: James Stevenson
Greenwillow, 2001. ISBN 0060294043.
Rating: 4 Stars
Grades: 2–9

      The author's father manages to keep his joy in collecting rocks through good and bad times until it eventually leads him to a fulfilling career.

Lowry, Lois. **Looking Back: A Book of Memories**
Houghton, 2000. ISBN 0385326998.
Rating: 4 Stars
Grades: 4–7

      Liberally illustrated with family photos, this book describes a series of memories inspired by the photos.

Marrin, Albert. **Unconditional Surrender: U. S. Grant and the Civil War**
Atheneum, 1994. ISBN 0689318375.
Rating: 4 Stars
Grades: 5–9

      Marrin's portrait brings to life the man who many, including Grant himself, viewed as a failure but who led the North to victory. Marrin's ability to use details while keeping the focus on the main events in a dramatic narrative style is outstanding.

Marrin, Albert. **Virginia's General**
Atheneum, 1994. ISBN 0689318383.
Rating: 4 Stars
Grades: 5–9

Using many quotes from other generals and his soldiers, Marrin shows Lee as the brave and extraordinary soldier that he was.

Mowat, Farley. **Never Cry Wolf: Amazing True Story of Life Among Arctic Wolves**
Back Bay Books, 2001. ISBN 0316881791.
Rating: 3 Stars
Grades: 5–9

Assigned fifty years ago by the Canadian Wildlife Service to find out why wolves were killing arctic caribou, Farley Mowat spent a summer studying wolf behavior. This account tells almost as much about him as it does about the wolves he studied for a summer.

Nelson, Marilyn. **Carver: A Life in Poems**
Front Street, 2001. ISBN 1886910537.
Rating: 3 Stars
Grades: 5–9

In fifty-nine stand-alone poems, Nelson covers the life and some of the deeds of George Washington Carver.

Paulsen, Gary. **Woodsong**
Scott Foresman, 1991. ISBN 0140349057.
Rating: 4 Stars
Grades: 5–9

Each chapter in this fascinating book provides another account of the author's experience with wild creatures and the sled dogs he loved. Many of the adventures revolve around the author's participation in the Iditarod.

Raschka, Chris. **Charlie Parker Played Be Bop**
Orchard, 1992. ISBN 0531070956.
Rating: 3 Stars
Grades: 2–9

A rhythmic text in varied formats and playful language recalls the rhythm and cadences of jazz musician, Charlie Parker.

Rockwell, Anne. **Only Passing Through: The Story of Sojourner Truth.** Illustrator: R. Gregory Christie
Knopf, 2000. ISBN 0679891862.
Rating: 3 Stars
Grades: 3–9

Remarkable text and stylized illustrations cover her early years up to her travels as an advocate for civil rights with an author's note telling us more about her life and work. The illustrations are remarkable.

Rylant, Cynthia. **When I Was Young in the Mountains.** Illustrator: Diane Goode

Dutton, 1993. ISBN 0140548750.

Rating: 4 Stars

Grades: PreK–3

This is so beautifully done and so popular as a picture book that we frequently forget it's an autobiography.

Say, Allen. **Grandfather's Journey**

Houghton, 1993. ISBN 0395570352.

Rating: 4 Stars

Grades: PreK–3

In this beautifully done picture-book biography is the story of the author's grandfather's search for the place where he felt completely at home.

Schroeder, Alan. **Minty: A Story of Young Harriet Tubman.** Illustrator: Jerry Pinkney

Puffin, 2000. ISBN 014056196X.

Rating: 3 Stars

Grades: 2–6

Beautifully illustrated, this book tells of the young rebellious slave, Minty, who grew up to become Harriet Tubman.

Sis, Peter. **Starry Messenger**

Farrar, 1996. ISBN 0374371911.

Rating: 3 Stars

Grades: 3–9

This biography of Galileo is a startlingly beautiful book in which words and illustrations twist about the pages giving new vantage points as the reader must turn the book to see them all.

Spinelli, Jerry. **Knots in My Yo-Yo String: The Autobiography of a Kid**

Knopf, 1998. ISBN 0679987916.

Rating: 3 Stars

Grades: 4–7

Spinelli writes of his childhood with the humor and sensitivity you'd expect from the author of Maniac Magee.

Stanley, Diane. **Cleopatra**

Morrow, 1994. ISBN 0688104134.

Rating: 3 Stars

Grades: 3–9

This is an excellent picture book biography of Cleopatra. There are maps and a lot of information about that time period, as well as information about ancient Egypt.

From *100+ Literacy Lifesavers: A Survival Guide for Librarians and Teachers K–12*
by Pamela S. Bacon and Tammy K. Bacon. Westport, CT: Libraries Unlimited. Copyright © 2009.

Warren, Andrea. **Orphan Train Rider: One Boy's True Story**
Houghton Mifflin, 1998. ISBN 0395913624.
Rating: 3 Stars
Grades: 4–9

Liberally illustrated, this story of one boy is placed within the context of the Orphan Train movement as a social experiment. It therefore becomes more than the story of one boy and his new life.

Lifesaver Tool #16.1

Biography Presentation Feedback Form

Name: _____   Date:_____

Presenter:_____

Biography Title:_____

Three facts I learned after reading the biography:

1. _____

2. _____

3. _____

The most important reason he or she is famous is:

_____

_____

Something I was surprised to learn during the presentation:

_____

_____

Lifesaver Tool #16.2

Biography Time Line

<u>Directions</u>: Record the five (5) most important events in the boxes below that you uncover during research.

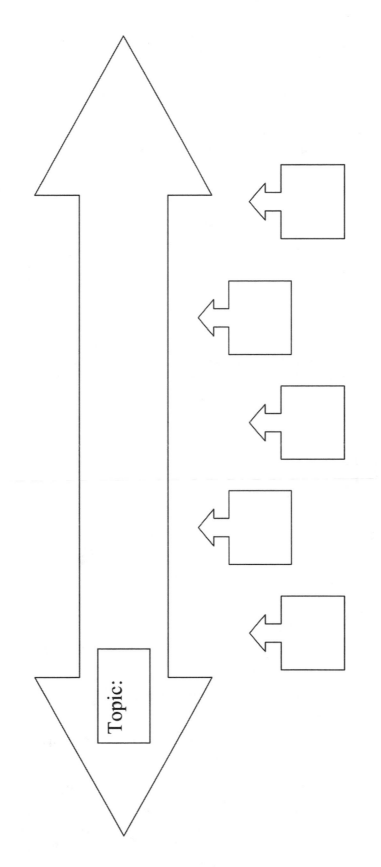

Topic:

Lifesaver Tool #16.3

Roses Are Red, Violets Are Blue, I Love Poems, How about You?

The great thing about poetry is that it naturally lends itself to all audiences, young and old. Because there is so much that can be done with poetry (including students' writing their own), this lifesaver will just keep you floating at the surface. Because poetry books abound, the media specialist's role will be critical in helping pull the best of the best. In addition, this is an excellent opportunity for the media specialist to bring in a guest poet to assist budding young poets in writing their own works.

Lifesaver Tips

- Don't ignore music as a poetry form for older students. Engagement and motivation is guaranteed!

- Poetry is a wonderful genre for interactive read-alouds, shared reading, and independent reading for primary students. After "making poems their own," students may work in stations to illustrate their favorites to be placed in poetry notebooks for future independent reading.

- Don't be afraid to introduce students to poems that don't rhyme, such as haiku (book recommendation: *One Leaf Rides the Wind*; refer to Lifesaver Tool #17) and acrostic poetry.

- Do use the opportunity to share quality poetry that stimulates emotion and feelings with students.

- For older students, use verse novels that provide a great opportunity for reader's theatre activities.

- Host Coffee House Nights and give older students a chance to read aloud their original poetry during open mic time.

- Ensure that poetry is an integral part of your daily program versus an add-on unit at the end of the year.

- Consider using themes to make poetry connections throughout the year.

- Use poetry often to build fluency.

- Assist students in using descriptive words and figurative language to enhance their poetry exposure.

- Select quality poetry (often found in picture books) to help students listen for the author's language (voice), which they can re-create in their own works.

- Host poetry slams with older students.

- Invite families for poetry celebrations to allow young poets a chance to present their revised, published poetry.

Lifesaver Tweaks

- Use the presentation screen for shared reading opportunities before working independently at stations. A great site for both activities is Scholastic's Playful Poetry (http://www.scholastic.com/earlylearner/parentandchild/literacy/playfulpoetry.htm.) This site models rereading for students (a critical reading strategy) and gives an assessment opportunity at the end).

- Use Shel Silverstein's amazing Web site for older students to check their comprehension of several famous poems after assigned readings. An interactive quiz is provided online (http://shelsilverstein.com/html/kidsgames.html).

- Use shared writing or interactive writing charts as a way to post rhyming word families so that students can access new vocabulary independently for use in creating their own original poems.

- Use KidPix as a way to integrate technology into your poetry lessons by using various forms of poetry (acrostics, shape poems, point of view poems, etc.). Media specialists can assist with the necessary technology to make these lessons come alive.

Lifesaver Trips #17

http://www.colegiobolivar.edu.co/library/primary_poetry.htm

This site provides one-stop shopping for colorful, animated primary poems that could be shown to a whole class on a presentation screen. The site also includes interactive activities that are perfect for younger students. Rhyming optional!

http://www.loc.gov/poetry/180/

The Poetry 180 site provides high school students with a poem a day by Poet Laureate Billy Collins.

http://www.kn.pacbell.com/wired/fil/pages/listpoetryde.html

This Internet Hotlist on Poetry ("Pounce on Poetry") includes awesome links to famous poets for all of you "cool cats"!

http://www.abcteach.com/Contributions/HaikuContest.htm

Invite students to read haikus written by former contest winners at this amazing site!

Haiku for You!

Name_____

1. Read *One Leaf Rides the Wind* by Celeste Mannis.
2. Talk to your partner about your favorite haiku in the story.
3. Brainstorm ideas about something in nature that inspires you!
4. Write your own haiku in the space below.
5. Check it with your partner and the teacher or media specialist.
6. Illustrate your haiku.
7. Add it to your poetry notebook.
8. Be ready to share it!

Haiku Reminder:

5 syllables–7 syllables–5 syllables

Title_____

Line 1_____

Line 2_____

Line 3_____

Lifesaver Tool #17

Get Real: Using Nonfiction and Informational Books

When many teachers and media specialists are asked about their favorite genre, many will answer "fiction." Because fictional books can be fun to read-aloud, invitational, and easy-to-understand (as well as colorful and visually stimulating), they are usually picked first off the shelf. "Michigan State University education researcher Nell Duke found in a study published in 2000 that first graders were exposed to an average of only 3.6 minutes of informational text per day. Students in lower socioeconomic groups fared even worse, with less than two minutes of such exposure per day" (http://education.uncc.edu/kdwood/Duke%20informational%20text.pdf). Although Duke notes later in the article that he believes that nonfiction reading has increased in the primary grades, many feel that focus is still needed in the nonfiction ocean of books. Some teachers at the secondary level tend to rely too heavily on their textbooks and too little on supplementary materials. The media specialist can help fill the gap by providing teachers with content-rich materials and taking the lead on modeling the use of nonfiction materials.

Lifesaver Tips

- Emphasize key elements of nonfiction/informational books: table of contents, index, headings, maps, illustrations, charts, bold and bulleted type, and glossary.

- Consider beginning this unit with a compare–contrast activity of a fiction and nonfiction book on the same topic.

- Have students assist with writing questions about a topic of interest that will be uncovered in the nonfiction genre.

- Offer students choice in nonfiction books. Choice encourages motivation.

- Model specific reading strategies and unique characteristics of nonfiction books. For example, navigating a map, using a table of contents, checking out an index, reading charts and graphs, making questions out of subheadings, and so on.

- Use nonfiction books as a way to teach the difficult skill of cause and effect with young readers.

- Use graphic organizers to help readers make sense of nonfiction text and to teach or reinforce key skills, such as finding main ideas or solving problems with textual responses.

- Use nonfiction texts to teach important skills, such as sequencing, to primary students by researching and drawing life cycles of pumpkins or apples.

- Utilize think-alouds while modeling the reading of nonfiction texts.

- Make reading–writing connections.

- Use questions from all levels of Bloom's Taxonomy.

- Use all types of nonfiction texts and books (dictionaries, atlases, picture books, informational books, etc.).

- Offer magazines and newspapers as supplementary nonfiction choices.

- Lifesaver Tools #18.1 and #18.2 provide worksheets for students to use both before and after reading.

Lifesaver Tweaks

- Utilize learning stations as a time to observe students working in guided practice groups with nonfiction texts.

- Have older students make audiotapes of informational books for ease of use by younger students.

- Model Internet research on the presentation screen to teach key reading strategies in the nonfiction genre.

- Use the "read to find out" method with primary students in guided reading groups to check comprehension and monitor understanding.

- Use echo reading as a chance to model fluency. (It's just as important with nonfiction as it is with fiction.)

- Explicitly teach key features of nonfiction when providing students with the book introduction at guided reading groups.

- Use nonfiction texts that are the most familiar to students. For example, Web pages offer the most up-to-date nonfiction material. Teachers and media specialists need to check out the Web sites they or their students use very carefully.

Lifesaver Trip #18

http://www.ncte.org/pubs/chron/highlights/126049.htm

Find specific strategies for using nonfiction with primary students (as well as research-based information on its importance) at this site.

http://dadtalk.typepad.com/cybils/2007/10/nonfiction-pict.html

Find the Cybil's Award Winners here for winning books in all genres (the Children and Young Adult Bloggers' Literary Awards). This exciting site offers the first Internet awards for books nominated by people like you and me (actually anyone with an Internet address can participate). Exercise *your* right to vote!

Get Real!
Nonfiction Summary Sheet for Shared Writing

I wonder …	I learned …

Lifesaver Tool #18.1

Get Real!
Using Nonfiction and Informational Books

Book Title:_____

Before Reading	**After Reading**

Questions	Answers

Literacy Lifesaver #19

Stranger Than Fiction!

Lifesaver Tips

- Explicitly teach various types of fiction novels, such as fantasy fiction, historical fiction, realistic fiction, and science fiction (see Lifesaver Tool 19.3).

- Explicitly teach the key elements of fiction: plot, setting, theme, character, and conflict.

- Explicitly teach figurative language with fiction choices, such as similes, metaphors, author's tone, foreshadowing, symbols, and so on.

- Invite students to compare and contrast historical fiction to realistic fiction.

- Use artifacts as primary sources from nonfiction books whenever possible to bring life to the books.

- Remember that science fiction is usually at a much higher reading level, but students can delve into them with supporting resources (help, media center specialist!).

- Do use the tried-and-true classics (we all love them), but ask your media specialist to help you dive into contemporary fiction titles to tie in the interests of today's teens.

- Use the literature circle model (see Literacy Lifesaver #41) as a way to offer students fiction choices.

- Use your media center to help you find webquests, online quizzes, and supplemental materials that are all available online (usually for free!).

- Use the Scholastic Reading Counts (SRC) or Accelerated Reader (AR) quizzes to assess comprehension. This is another great collaboration opportunity between the classroom and the media center.

- Collaborate with the media center specialist to review logs and discover what genre needs extra emphasis.

Lifesaver Tweaks

- Don't overlook the use of big books, wordless picture books, or concept books as opportunities to teach and model reading strategies for primary students.

- Use resources such as dictionaries and thesauruses to model word solving at the primary level.

- Utilize children's writing from writing workshops as a way to model elements of fiction.

- Use historical fiction as a way to meet social studies standards through interactive read-alouds at the primary level.

- Have students keep reading logs during self-selected reading as a way to monitor genres that students self-select (see Lifesaver Tool #19.1 for primary and Lifesaver Tool #19.2 for secondary)

Lifesaver Trips #19

http://teacher.scholastic.com/lessonrepro/lessonplans/instructor/social1.htm#tips

Want to know why and how to teach historical fiction? Find out here!

http://www.abcteach.com/directory/reading_comprehension/grades_24/fictional/

Find a clickable annotated list of realistic titles for grades 2–4 with activities and comprehension questions at the click of a mouse.

http://info.infosoup.org/lists/RealisticFictionAll.asp?BooklistID=73

Find a nicely put together list of realistic fiction books focusing on teen problems here.

Reading Log

Name_____

Date	Book Title	Genre
		F = Fiction, N = Nonfiction

_____

_____

_____

_____

_____

_____

_____

_____

_____

_____

_____

_____

_____

_____

_____

_____

_____

_____

_____

_____

_____

_____

_____

_____

_____

_____

Lifesaver Tool #19.1

Reading Log

Name_____

Week of_____

Title_____	Pages_____		Reading minutes Genre
M Summary or Reflections_____			Teacher Signature
_____			
_____			
_____			

Title_____	Pages_____		Reading minutes Genre
T Summary or Reflections_____			Teacher Signature
_____			
_____			
_____			

Title_____	Pages_____		Reading minutes Genre
W Summary or Reflections_____			Teacher Signature
_____			
_____			
_____			

Title_____	Pages_____		Reading minutes Genre
T Summary or Reflections_____			Teacher Signature
_____			
_____			
_____			

Title_____	Pages_____		Reading minutes Genre
F Summary or Reflections_____			Teacher Signature
_____			
_____			
_____			

SF = science fiction, FF = fantasy fiction, B = biography, P = poetry, HF = historical fiction, RF = realistic fiction, N = nonfiction

Lifesaver Tool #19.2

Genre Study Key Elements

Fiction (historical and realistic)

- Stories centered around the basis of a partially historical situation

- A novel set in a historical period

- Stories that take place in modern times

- Characters are involved in events that could happen

Fantasy
Contains elements that are not realistic:

- talking animals

- magical powers

- often set in a medieval universe

- possibly involving mythical beings

Mystery
A novel involving:

- strangeness

- solving a puzzling event or situation

- something unknown

- solving a crime

- centered around a person who investigates wrongdoing

- centered around a person or persons employed to obtain secret information

Science Fiction

- Stories that often tell about science and technology of the future

- Involving partially true fiction laws or theories of science

- Settings

  - in the future
  - in space
  - in a different world
  - in a different universe or dimension

Lifesaver Tool #19.3

Literacy Lifesaver #20

Go Play!

When it comes to performances, it often doesn't feel like "play" for the teacher or media specialist. Actually, plays are hard work to pull off, but worth it in the end. Most people, regardless of age, remember a special school play or performance as a memorable and rewarding learning experience. (Pam played John Adams in the sixth-grade play. I actually beat out a future boyfriend for the guy's part.) Reader's Theatre offers chances for all students to become actors and actresses on the small classroom stage while allowing the teacher and media specialist to become directors of reading strategies.

Lifesaver Tips

- Explicitly teach key elements of plays (see http://blog.wku.edu/podcasts/Waters_ENG200_Drama.ppt#12 for key vocabulary and a great PowerPoint presentation).

- Use Reader's Theatre as often as you can. New to Reader's Theatre? Go to http://www.stemnet.nf.ca/CITE/langrt.htm#What.

- Keep in mind the learning styles and personalities of your students when acting out plays. Some of the shyer students, for example, might be awesome set designers. Other quiet students may "shine" when role-playing and provided with a mask or costume.

- Don't forget that the media center can become an awesome stage.

- Assist students with writing their own short plays (some online sites, such as www.teenink.com, have Writer's Workshops for dramatists and places for submission of original plays).

- Create organizers to hold scripts and plays (a three-ring binder works great, and the pocket allows for storage of notes and highlighters).

- Take students to see plays whenever possible.

- Collaborate with the art and music teacher for props and background music to make your play come alive. Don't feel obligated to act out every play; sometimes students just like to be assigned a part in class and read it aloud (even secondary students like corny Burger King crowns when playing the part of Oedipus).

- Allow students to be directors and critique the performance (see Lifesaver Tool #20.1 for a primary rubric and Lifesaver Tool #20.2 for a secondary rubric).

Lifesaver Tweaks

- Remember the most important strategies to implement Reader's Theatre at the primary level are repetition, repetition, repetition (get the point?) and rehearsal (practice, practice, practice). See Lifesaver Tool #20.3 for five steps to implement Reader's Theatre in the classroom or library.

- Use tongue twisters to build fluency and critical enunciation skills.

- Assist younger students with using scripts as shared reading opportunities and model the use of a highlighter to mark lines.

- Utilize learning stations at the primary level as a time to practice roles in the drama station.

Lifesaver Trip #20

http://www.aaronshep.com/stories/index.html

Click on Aaron's World of Stories to find scripts and tips for Reader's Theater (all ages).

Reader's Theatre Response Rubric

1. Were the words easy to understand?

        Yes   Sometimes   No

2. Was the actor loud enough?

        Yes   Sometimes   No

3. Did the actor use expression?

        Yes   Sometimes   No

4. Did the actor make the character "come alive"?

        Yes   Sometimes   No

5. Did the actor remember the lines?

        Yes   Sometimes   No

6. What was your favorite character and why?

Lifesaver Tool #20.1 (Primary Grades)

Reader's Theatre Response Rubric

Please listen carefully and respectfully to the dramatic performance today. As you listen to the performance, consider the following items and "grade" them below with a **+, v,** or **–**.

1. Clarity of **voice** (Articulation—words were clear and easy to understand)

2. Voice **projection** (Loudness, or volume, was high enough to be heard at the back of the room)

3. **Voice** inflection (Voices rose and fell as in real life expression)

4. **Believability** of character

5. **Practice and timing** (parts read smoothly without extra pauses)

6. Who was your favorite character and why?

Lifesaver Tool #20.2 (Secondary Grades)

Play Around with Reader's Theatre

Prepare a script.

Let students adapt the script (as needed).

Assign parts.

Yell "ready, set" and rehearse.

Action!

Stage it—perform!!

Lifesaver Tool #20.3

Lifesaver Notes

_____

_____

_____

_____

_____

_____

_____

_____

_____

_____

_____

_____

_____

_____

_____

_____

_____

_____

_____

_____

_____

Lifesaver Notes

Chapter 3

Reading Strategies (Before–During–After)

Literacy Lifesaver #21

Q & A . . . What Do You Say?

If you've got questions, we'll find answers! Our version of the basic K-W-L (What I KNOW, What I WANT to know, What I LEARNED) chart simplifies the strategy into a quick two-step process chart. This activity can be done as a whole group, small guided reading group, or even individually—whichever best suits the needs of your class. The media specialist is the perfect person to provide the answers or to point you in the right direction to the reference section. Check it out!

Lifesaver Tips

- Use the handout provided (see Lifesaver Tool #21) for a quick before-reading activity.

- Use a large spiral-bound chart (turn the chart upright like a book with questions on the left side of the spiral and answers on the right) to set up the chart, as shown in Lifesaver Tool #21. This is a great way for the teacher or librarian to model what the students will do independently in their own notebooks.

- Use the left side of the chart for before reading; use the right side of the chart for after-reading discussion.

- Save completed Q & A charts in a three-ring binder for quick future reference.

- Complete the answer side of the chart in the media center where students can participate in a scavenger hunt search for answers.

- Complete the Q & A chart in small cooperative groups, then have groups share jigsaw-style to ensure knowledge is equally shared by all.

- Consider using two colors of dry-erase markers on the whiteboard to easily distinguish later additions and changes to the chart. For example, at the end of the lesson, there may be questions you want to add that are still unanswered.

Lifesaver Tweaks

- Intermediate and secondary students can obviously complete the chart on their own; primary students will need scribes.

- Use Post-It notes or thematic cutouts (Ellison machines work great) to place individual questions on the Q & A chart. This ensures participation by all students. Don't worry about repetition (you may even want to group like answers to see informal data results).

- Copy the tool onto a transparency for small-group presentations using the overhead (meet those speaking standards while building prior knowledge—kill two birds with one stone!).

- Create the chart using Lifesaver Trip #21. Use the SmartBoard with the chart for a totally interactive learning experience.

- Ask the media specialist to work with students on basic reference tools, such as dictionaries, encyclopedias, and thesauruses.

Lifesaver Trip #21

http://www.teach-nology.com/web_tools/graphic_org/kwl

The classic meets the modern on this activity. The traditional K-W-L chart goes wild and crazy in an up-to-date technology format. By simply typing in a quick teacher name, subject, and topic into the pre-generated template, you have a professional-looking tool in a matter of seconds.

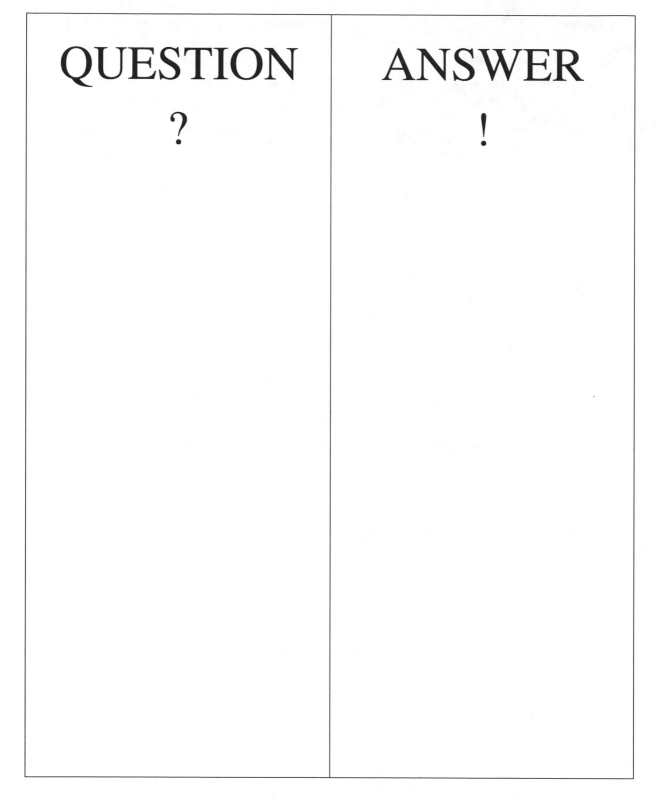

QUESTION ?	ANSWER !

Lifesaver Tool #21

Literacy Lifesaver #22

Walk the Line

Looking for a fun, interactive way to get students thinking about the book before they start reading? Instead of "Listen Up!" (we say that often enough, don't we?), this time say, "Line Up!" Like Literacy Lifesaver #21, this lifesaver strategy can also be used as an after-reading strategy.

Lifesaver Tips

- Put a tape line out in the hall or in an empty area of the classroom or media center.

- Prepare a list of five value statements or opinion-based sentences (the number can be more or less depending on the content of book and level of students). Ask students to line up, placing the tops of their shoes "on the line."

- Read aloud the statements on your list (see Lifesaver Tool #22).

- Direct students to take a step forward if they agree with the statement or opinion.

- Direct students to take a step backward if they disagree with the statement or opinion.

Lifesaver Tweaks

- Tally the number of students who agree and disagree, then do the activity again, this time *after* reading the book. Discuss whether the students' beliefs or opinions changed as a result of reading or whether new learning took place.

- Encourage students to make their own decisions to make sure they don't let their peers influence their beliefs!

- Practice "Walk the Line" with one basic statement to which all students can relate (for example, "A good friend should always tell the truth!"). Practice, practice, practice before trying longer "Walk the Line" activities.

Lifesaver Trip #22

http://www.uen.org/Lessonplan/preview.cgi?LPid=15238

The Human Line Plot takes the "Walk the Line" activity up the charts (literally!) as students "plot" to use their bodies to form physical human graphs. Although the as-is version is not recommended for primary students, intermediate and secondary students will want to take a number and stand in line for this fun activity!

Walk the Line
Tally Chart

Statement #1:	# Agree:	# Disagree:
Statement #2:		
Statement #3:		
Statement #4:		
Statement #5:		

Lifesaver Tool #22

Literacy Lifesaver #23

Book Introductions: Have We Met?

One of the most powerful ways to prepare students for a read aloud or simply for success with independent reading is a strong book introduction. As with all activities, it is important to be clear and concise and to connect students directly to the text. Whether the book is introduced by the media specialist or the classroom teacher, students will immediately "sea" the difference after participating in this experience.

Lifesaver Tips

- Look through the text and place Post-It notes to label key components for meaning, structure, and visual.

- Write out a short introduction that includes the basics of the story.

- Note key story elements, such as plot, setting, characters, and the problems (conflicts) in the text.

- Choose words and elements that you specifically want to bring out prior to the lesson and what you might leave for the students to problem solve during the read (see Lifesaver Tool #23).

- Keep a "teacher copy" of the student book with Post-Its and notes attached for quick, ready-made lessons for future use.

Lifesaver Tweaks

- Ask the media specialist to provide book introductions for special stories, such as author studies, research or topic studies, and award-winning books.

- Provide opportunities for students to present book introductions for stories that they have enjoyed and want to recommend.

- Utilize collaborative planning sheets with other grade-level teachers to divide and conquer, allowing you to keep your head above water!

- Use the book introduction strategy with all books whenever possible, but especially with social studies and science texts to help prepare students to be successful with reading across the content areas.

Lifesaver Trip #23

http://www.arliteracymodel.com/pdf/development/Book%20Introductions,%20Powerful%20Tools%20for%20Powerful%20Thinkin.pdf

This site features a PowerPoint presentation containing critical background knowledge for book introductions at the primary level. Although the PowerPoint is based on a Reading Recovery classroom, the information is valuable to all.

http://www.sparknotes.com/

Need free online study guides? Look no further! Surf here anytime you need preview or introductory material on a book before you do a read-aloud or start a novel project. What a novel idea (pun intended)!

Guided Reading Observational Assessment Tool

Story:_____

Story Elements Taught:

_____

_____

_____

_____

Vocabulary Words:

_____   Specifically Teach   Monitor/Problem Solving

_____   Specifically Teach   Monitor/Problem Solving

_____   Specifically Teach   Monitor/Problem Solving

_____   Specifically Teach   Monitor/Problem Solving

_____   Specifically Teach   Monitor/Problem Solving

Student Name(s):

Observational Notes during Guided Reading

Literacy Lifesaver #24

Break the Code!

The most important reading strategies, in our opinion, are those you use during reading. After you've done some exciting prereading strategies to engage students in the text, elicit prior knowledge, and motivate them to want to read the book, it's time to get after it and start the reading. Now what do you do? Well, there are a "sea" of choices available, but this lifesaver focuses on using coding during reading to improve comprehension so readers dive in and understand what they read.

Lifesaver Tips

- Use Lifesaver Tools #24.1 and #24.2 to help students learn to code (mark the text) while they read.

- Model, model, model. You can't use this strategy too much before you let students dive in and use it on their own.

- Begin by modeling the strategies with a great read-aloud book. Use the stop and think aloud strategy first to help students understand the coding process.

- Now, go one step further by showing the students what you code on your Post-It note while you read. Showing relevant examples is key. Don't go overboard at first—less is more, so model one code at a time.

- Next, use the "fishbowl" approach and let capable students model inside the "bowl" for other students (who are outside the "bowl" looking in before they go fishing!). You will need to do some critical observing while students are reading to choose the best "swimmers" for this activity.

- Allow students to see adults utilizing this strategy. The media specialist is a wonderful resource here to model the strategy for students. Collaboration is key, though, so ensure that the coding marks of the teacher and the media specialist are the same.

Lifesaver Tweaks

- Start this process with primary students by utilizing small guided reading groups with a high level of teacher support during the read.

- Consider putting students in small, heterogeneous groups while having one student act as the recorder.

- Remember that primary students may only be able to code with a question mark or exclamation mark (refer to Lifesaver Tool #24.1).

- Use color coding at the intermediate and secondary levels. Color coding can allow you to easily track types of questions (questions in red for comprehension or questions in green for vocabulary, etc.).

Lifesaver Trip #24

http://eds.ucsd.edu/courses/eds361a/FA07/lect3.ppt#1

This site features a wonderful PowerPoint presentation that is a perfect tool to use for staff development and collaboration of many key strategies. Ideally, this is a presentation that the teacher and the media specialist could give to staff during a professional development day. The PowerPoint presentation also includes an awesome idea: the wondering cube! Go to the site to read all about it!

http://www.middleweb.com/ReadWrkshp/RWdownld/01CL_CurrMap.pdf

This site is a little overwhelming at first, but it is one of the best resources to use to map out your literacy plan when teaching a book. The six-week detailed unit plan for reading informational texts (which could be easily adapted for fictional texts) is a step-by-step curriculum map for content literacy. There's a lot of information to dive into, but the site provides an intentional way to ensure your literacy goals are being met. Dive in carefully and wear your scuba suit (doubtless, you'll be going under before you surface with great ideas for your next book unit!).

Primary "Post" Office

Copy this tool and cut out—or (better yet!) make up sticky notes with the codes!

```
? = I don't understand

! = I loved this part!

WW = Wonderful Word

AL = Author's Language

Name_____
```

Lifesaver Tool #24.1

Break the Code!
Kid-Friendly Codes to Use during Reading

Code	Meaning	Mastered
!	Wow! That part rocks!	
?	Huh? I dunno.	
*	Don't forget!	
B-S	Book to Self	
B-B	Book to Book	
B-W	Book to World	
B-F	Book to Friend	
B-M	Book to Movie	

Code:

B-S: The book reminds me of myself. (Note: secondary students love the B-S code—I'm sure you can imagine why! They actually enjoyed marking their text with this one!).

B-B The book reminds me of another book I've read.

B-W: The book reminds me of something going on in the world around me.

B-F: The book reminds me of my best friend (intermediate and secondary students prefer this one to the B-S code—it's much easier to think of a "friend" instead of themselves!).

B-M: The book reminds me of a movie (or television show) I've seen.

Mastered:

Use this column as a checklist to mark when students have mastered the strategy!

Note: Adapted from *Strategies That Work* (Harvey & Goudvis, 2000).

Lifesaver Tool #24.2

Prepare to Repair: Tools for Working through the Words

OK, you've done some great prereading strategies, and students are motivated to read the book. You've modeled and practiced text coding (see Literacy Lifesaver #24), but you're still not sure students are really "getting it." What do you do? You get it "write" by using words to clarify meaning during reading!

Lifesaver Tips

- Model the process of reading to find out information and logging the answers. Students can then follow suit using their reader's notebooks, on sticky notes, on personal student bookmarks, and so on.

- Stop during reading for a quick free-write. Simply allowing a few minutes for students to process what they have read can be a great comprehension builder.

- Until students can learn the strategy on their own, have them stop at various times during their reading to answer questions on a reading guide. Remember, it's helpful to list page numbers and then gradually release responsibility as students become more competent readers.

- Use cooperative learning group roles for writing responses. For example, a recorder can list information on a large chart for the group (just remember to change roles so that all students have experiences with writing and recording).

- Have students "freeze" during reading, then discuss a point to add to a graphic organizer. When students "unfreeze," they can complete the graphic organizer. Again, with lots of modeling and practice, students will eventually be competent enough to stop or pause on their own during reading.

Lifesaver Tweaks

- Secondary students can write their own multiple-choice questions as they read. Making the quizzes builds comprehension, and the quizzes can easily be put into a computerized format (like Scholastic Reading Counts or Accelerated Reader). The media specialist can often assist your efforts in this area because he or she is usually the "head cheerleader" for these reading incentive programs.

- Break up text for longer books (passages) or when working with primary students. Have students stop at specific, predetermined spots and write a response (a sentence for primary, paragraph for secondary).

- Ask students to go back to their coding (see Literacy Lifesaver #24) and explain their codes. Lifesaver Tool #25.1 (primary) and Lifesaver Tool #25.2 (secondary) provide ready-to-use templates for this strategy.

- Provide time for primary students to read with partners, stopping verbally for pair share. Finally, record answers or responses on a shared writing chart.

- Read in the media center computer lab. Students can read and respond in writing using a word processing program or online graphic organizer.

Lifesaver Trip #25

**http://www.pde.state.pa.us/reading_writing/lib/reading_writing/
BEFORE-DURING-AFTER_READING_STRATEGIES.doc**

Go fish for some great writing activities here to use during reading (or before or after!).

Break the Code!

Text Code	Page #	Reason for Code
?		I don't understand . . .
!		I really liked the part when . . .
WW		A wonderful word I found was . . .

Lifesaver Tool #25.1

Text Code	Page #	Reason for Code

Lifesaver Tool #25.2

Literacy Lifesaver #26

Take Note: Using Reader's Notebooks

You've broken the code for students to make great connections while they read. You've used writing as a tool to make deeper meaning from text. This lifesaver provides one more great strategy—the Reader's Notebook.

Lifesaver Tips

- The Reader's Notebook is a way to help students gain deeper meaning as they interact with the text.

- Lifesaver Tool #26 offers a list of items to include in your Reader's Notebook. Obviously, this tool just touches the surface of what could be included in a quality notebook, but we hope this lifesaver will allow you to get your feet wet.

- Collaborate with the media specialist on how the Reader's Notebook can be a part of collaborative units and research projects.

- Help students become better readers with the Reader's Notebook by modeling the process of recording quality text responses, such as personal thoughts and feelings about passages of a book.

- Use retelling along with responding. Although retelling is more basic, the strategy is still useful, especially for struggling readers. Retelling and summarizing at the end of each page can be a valuable tool if practiced and modeled effectively. Then, when students have mastered the strategy, retelling (summarizing) can be a great after-reading assessment.

- Post lists of key questions and Reader's Notebook responses around the classroom (Fountas & Pinnell, 2001). For example, "What do you think is the author's message?" is a great response question that is directly tied to standards.

Lifesaver Tweaks

- Use the Reader's Notebook to help differentiate for the many levels of readers. This is a great piece to collaborate with the media specialist for students who are ready to start a new book or begin an individual research project before others have finished.

- Divide and conquer. Keep a group of readers with you who need additional modeling of Reader's Notebook strategies while the media specialist dives into guiding an enrichment group through a Reader's Notebook project.

- Primary students benefit from a shared reading chart that they can copy into their Reader's Notebook.

- Utilize interactive writing strategies with younger students to allow them to "share the pen" while creating a whole-class entry.

- Secondary students who are struggling readers also need support and modeling (although some students can work independently right away). Use the SmartBoard for interactive modeling whenever possible. (The media specialist can usually assist with SmartBoard implementation!)

Lifesaver Trip #26

http://ritter.tea.state.tx.us/gted/ReaStra.pdf

You've got to "sea" this amazing resource site that contains a great Reader's Notebook for all students but focuses on differentiating the needs of individual readers. Ready to use tools are included. Don't be fooled by the primary title—it's a diving board for all levels!

Reader's Notebook Checklist

Reading Goals ☐

Reading Records (Book Logs) ☐

Reading Genre Lists ☐

Reading Interests ☐

Reading Lists (To Reads) ☐

Reading Conference Notes ☐

Choosing Books Handouts ☐

Reading Response Questions ☐

Reading Project Handouts ☐

Book Talk Handouts ☐

Letter Writing Information ☐

Reading Quotes Pages ☐

Reading Vocabulary Pages ☐

Reflection Pages (Blank) ☐

Note: Make a Reader's Notebook out of any standard spiral-bound notebook. Just remember to leave the first page blank for a table of contents. It's a handy way to keep track of what's in there (and what's not!).

Other things to include:

Lifesaver Tool #26

From *100+ Literacy Lifesavers: A Survival Guide for Librarians and Teachers K–12* by Pamela S. Bacon and Tammy K. Bacon. Westport, CT: Libraries Unlimited. Copyright © 2009.

Literacy Lifesaver #27

Prepare to Repair: "Get It" Strategies

After students have finished a book or a story, it's critical to check comprehension. Did they "get it?" An easy way to answer this question is simply to give a test. The test scores tell you loud and clear whether you need to "prepare to repair." Next time, before moving on, use the following "get it" strategies to repair comprehension.

Lifesaver Tips

- **R**eread. Find out where you got confused.

- **E**xplore. Discover what would make sense using context clues.

- **P**air Up and Discuss. Choose a partner to ask questions, make predictions, and talk about the text.

- **A**ttack the word.

- **I**gnore. Skip and read on.

- **R**ead slower or faster.

Lifesaver Tweaks

- Reread. Model the strategy of starting back at the beginning of the sentence or at the point of confusion to repair meaning or word attack skills (primary). This strategy can also work with secondary students. Keep in mind, though, that when older students "reread," unfortunately, they are often just reading the text for the first time. Providing concentrated time for older students to read the text is critical (secondary).

- Explore. Students should always be taken back to the point of meaning. Prompt students often with, "Would that make sense?" (primary and secondary).

- Pair up and discuss. Use the "turn and talk" or "knee to knee" strategy with younger students to encourage oral language and comprehension skills during discussion (primary).

(Refer to the glossary and resources for more specific information about these strategies.) Use the "shoulder partner" or "pick a partner" strategy to help older students "get it" through discussion (secondary).

- Attack the word. Although some words can look big and overwhelming to younger students, encourage them to "work through the word" from the beginning, middle and end to word solve (primary). Older students can attack words by looking up the word in a dictionary or online at dictionary.com (secondary).

- Ignore. Younger students can be encouraged to skip the word and move on; this strategy can allow early readers to revert to context clues to get at meaning (primary). When students can't arrive at meaning after using context clues, encourage students to mark the point of confusion with a Post-It note to revisit after reading (primary and secondary).

- Read slower or faster. Students often try to read too fast (secondary) or too slow (primary). Adjusting the reading rate is one way to repair comprehension.

- ! The media specialist can be a critical member of the "repair team." By helping students choose "just right" books and working with students on the repair strategies during sustained silent reading in the media center, they'll "get it" in no time! Lifesaver Tool #27 is a poster of the REPAIR strategies for easy reference!

Lifesaver Trip #27

http://www.readinglady.com/mosaic/tools/Fix-Up%20Strategies%20 bookmarks%20by%20Cherie.pdf

This site features a great bookmark of other "get it" strategies by the well-known Reading Lady! You'll want to be sure to bookmark more of her resources on your computer!

REPAIR STRATEGIES: READ IT AND "GET IT"

Reread. Find out where you got confused.

Explore. Discover what would make sense using context clues.

Pair Up and Discuss. Choose a partner to ask questions, make predictions, and talk about the text.

Attack the word.

Ignore. Skip and read on.

Read slower or faster.

Read It Again!

Your students have finished with their first read of the text. What do you do now? As you know, one of the keys to reading comprehension is fluency. To keep your students afloat, use the READ strategies below. They'll have so much fun with these reading strategies, they won't even complain that they have to "read it again!"

Lifesaver Tips

- **R**ead chorally

- **E**cho read

- **A**ct it out with reader's theatre

- **D**ivide into partners

- Choral reading is a great way to help students develop fluency in their reading. Divide the text into parts with the teacher or media specialist reading part of the text and the students joining in a shared, choral reading of favorite parts. Lifesaver Tool #28 provides a choral reading assessment tool.

- Echo reading allows for all students to be successful. By modeling reading and having students repeat the sentence or passage, it allows students to "stand on the teacher's shoulders" to read with expression and discover unknown words.

- Reader's theatre allows students to use their creativity by taking parts of the story to read and act out. It allows for all of the fun of a play without the props and headaches! The media specialist, another class, or parents can make for a great audience. In addition, the media center is a great place for a more formal presentation stage with built-in support and a captive audience.

- Partner reading works well when students are appropriately matched. Heterogeneous partners work best when students are reading together without much teacher direction. Partner reading is a great after-reading strategy to provide struggling readers with needed support. This is also a great time for a teacher to listen in for some observational assessment to monitor comprehension.

Lifesaver Tweaks

- Practice and model strategies with secondary students. Even though echo reading and choral reading can seem "juvenile" at first, when used intentionally and practiced, this strategy has merit and validity for older students.

- Beware! High school students will often "act out" (not in a good way!) when not given highly structured activities and clear expectations.

- Consider having older students present to younger students and then do some partner reading together.

- Partner reading at the intermediate and high school levels requires close monitoring, proximity, and sometimes the accountability of a written response sheet.

Lifesaver Trip #28

http://www.teachingheart.net/readerstheater.htm

http://www.aaronshep.com/rt/RTE.html

Check out these wonderful resources for reader's theatre scripts for all grade levels!

Choral Reading Student Assessment Tool

Student's Name_____

Date_____

The student used expression during the reading.	Yes	No	Partially
The student read fluently.	Yes	No	Partially
The student's body language was confident.	Yes	No	Partially
The student read loudly enough.	Yes	No	Partially
The student was well prepared.	Yes	No	Partially

Comments:

Lifesaver Tool #28

From *100+ Literacy Lifesavers: A Survival Guide for Librarians and Teachers K–12*
by Pamela S. Bacon and Tammy K. Bacon. Westport, CT: Libraries Unlimited. Copyright © 2009.

After the Fact—Ideas That Bloom!

After students have read and reread the text, it is time to think about extending their learning to move them forward in their comprehension. This also allows the use of Bloom's Taxonomy to meet the needs of the various learners in your classroom. With the support of the media specialist, you can divide and conquer to collaborate on extension activities that can be varied to better meet individual needs.

Lifesaver Tips

Use the various levels of Bloom's Taxonomy as stems for after-reading extensions. Following are a few of the possibilities to help you "dive in"!

- Knowledge—Retell the story in order with detail.

- Comprehension—Summarize the main events and explain how the problem in the story was solved.

- Application—What would you have done if you were the main character?

- Analysis—Which part of the story was the most interesting for you? Why?

- Synthesis—Create a new ending or title for the story. Explain your reasons for your choice.

Lifesaver Tweaks

- Students may do the previous activity verbally or in a writing or drawing based on the time you have available and the level of your students.

- Utilize the media specialist as a second person for observational assessment to "listen in" as the students verbally answer the questions.

- Model each of the strategies clearly, intentionally, and explicitly before assessing students and expecting independence.

- Don't be afraid to vary the questions to the level of the student. Knowledge questions can be challenging for struggling readers, whereas analysis and synthesis will keep your accelerated students thinking.

- Use the assessment rubric to document your observations (Lifesaver Tool #29).

Lifesaver Trip #29:

http://www.ode.state.or.us/teachlearn/subjects/elarts/reading/literacy/ primarycompafter.ppt#1

Although listed as strategies for primary grades, these ideas cross over to all grade levels. The examples presented are exemplary and provide teachers and media specialists support for after-reading strategies.

http://www.geocities.com/blue_spruce2003/pdfs/readingstrategies2003.pdf

Check out this wonderful resource of picture books with before, during, and after strategy suggestions!

http://www.greece.k12.ny.us/instruction/ela/6-12/Reading/Reading%20 Strategies/reading%20strategies%20index.htm

Intermediate and secondary teachers will appreciate this resource site, which includes a variety of strategies with clear descriptions and relevant examples.

Name _____

Story _____

Date _____

After the Fact: Reading Rubric

Circle the areas assessed and write comments in the space provided.

- Knowledge: The student was able to retell the story in order with detail.

    yes   no   partially

    Comments:

- Comprehension: The student was able to summarize the main events and explain how the problem in the story was solved.

    yes   no   partially

    Comments:

- Application: The student was able to say what he or she would have done if he or she were the main character.

    yes   no   partially

    Comments:

- Analysis: The student was able to share which part of the story was the most interesting for him or her and to explain why.

    yes   no   partially

    Comments:

- Synthesis: The student was able to create a new ending or title (or both) for the story and to explain his or her reasons for the choice.

    yes   no   partially

    Comments:

Lifesaver Tool #29

Get on a Roll with Reading Strategies!

This lifesaver, featuring the cubing strategy, is a great after-reading strategy. What's even better is that the strategy also works just as well for before reading and during reading! Your students will get on a roll with these reading strategies and improve their comprehension. The fun, hands-on strategy works with any book or content!

Lifesaver Tips

- The cubing template (Lifesaver Tool #30.1) is blank so that it can easily be written on to customize this activity for your needs. (See the following Web site for more information on cubing: http://forpd.ucf.edu/strategies/stratCubing.html.)

- Use the cubing strategy with any content area. For example, by making cubes with vocabulary words, you have a fun, hands-on way to practice vocabulary. By making cubes with story parts, you can review key elements of a story. The choices are endless, and you and your students will be on a roll!

Lifesaver Tweaks

- The tweaks for Literacy Lifesaver #30 are included on the tools. (Lifesaver Tool #30.1 is a cube template; Lifesaver Tool #30.2 provides a list of reading comprehension questions that you can use to customize your cube.)

- Use the cubes during extra time in the media center. Because the cubes are so light-weight, they're easy to take with you.

- The media specialist may even want to make some customized research cubes focusing on media vocabulary or research topics.

Lifesaver Trip #30

http://www.saskschools.ca/~qvss/curriculum/readcomp.htm

Surf here to find a variety of reading strategies. You can get on a roll with cubing or dive into other great strategies!

Get on a Roll! Cubing Template

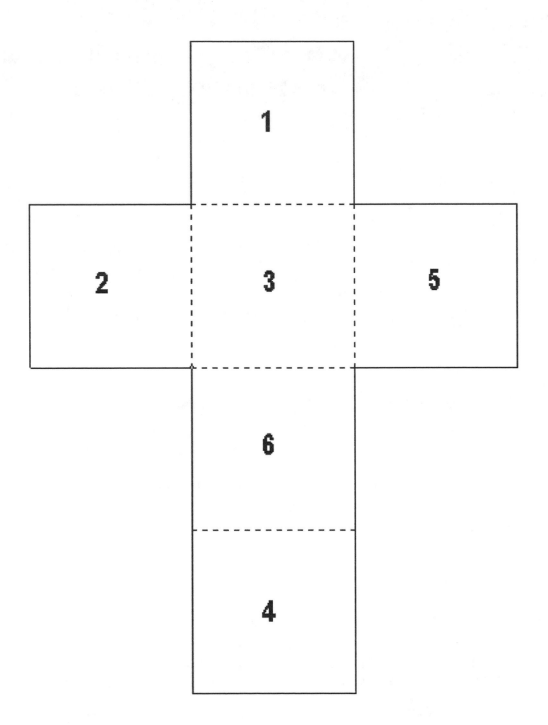

Lifesaver Tool #30.1

Get on a Roll!
Cubing Questions to Improve Reading Comprehension

Primary Questions:

1. Who was the main character?

2. Where did the story happen?

3. What was the story *mostly* about?

4. When did the story happen?

5. Why was the character _____?

6. How did the author solve the problem in the story?

Secondary Questions:

1. Who was the antagonist in the story? Who was the protagonist?

2. Where (and when) did the story take place? Include setting details.

3. What was the main idea of the story?

4. When did the resolution take place? Did the character change as a result?

5. What was the author's tone?

6. How were the conflicts in the story resolved?

Media Center Questions:

1. Who is the author of _____?

2. Where are the _____ books located?

3. What would you find in the reference section?

4. When is the media center open after school?

5. Why did Dewey come up with his system for categorizing books?

6. How many books can you check out? How long can you keep them?

Lifesaver Tool #30.2

Lifesaver Notes

_____

_____

_____

_____

_____

_____

_____

_____

_____

_____

_____

_____

_____

_____

_____

_____

_____

_____

_____

_____

_____

Chapter 4

Visualization Activities

Reader's Note: Unlike the format in the other chapters, this chapter is unique in that it begins with five primary lifesavers, followed by secondary lifesavers. The tweaks for both are how to adapt the lifesavers to meet the needs of intermediate students. Because the content of literature circles varies so widely, we felt this format would be more user-friendly and specific to each audience.

Literacy Lifesaver #31

"Sea" the Difference

If you're looking for a way to help your students better understand what they're reading, they've got to see it to believe it. Making mental pictures or playing movies in their mind is a technique that can be modeled and specifically taught by the classroom teacher or library media specialist. Too often we assume students already have these visualization skills, but they often don't. It's not too late to get the cameras rolling—ready, set, action!

Lifesaver Tips

- Have students close their eyes while you read aloud descriptive picture books or text passages.

- Use Post-It notes to mark specific parts of the book that best lend themselves to visualization. Leave Post-Its on the book after you've finished with it to save valuable planning time for next year (note: this strategy doesn't work well when it's a library book!).

- Create a class chart (or word wall) of adjectives and describing words that are interesting and fun to visualize.

- Use video clips following the modeling and instruction of visualization techniques to compare and contrast the book, the students' "mind's eye" version, and the movie version.

- A Venn diagram (see Lifesaver Tool #31) works well for either individual or class compare-contrast charts.

- As always, build prior knowledge whenever possible to help students create more detailed, accurate mental models.

- Model, model, model the visualization strategy.

- Use the think-aloud strategy to help students "picture" what you're thinking.

- Ask the media specialist to pull especially graphic picture books or novels that highlight descriptive and eloquent writing.

Lifesaver Tweaks

- Secondary: Students may resist closing their eyes. For this strategy to be effective, students must close their eyes and concentrate on the read-aloud. By enforcing a little "shut eye" immediately, the benefits will be eye opening later.

- Primary: When beginning to use this strategy with primary students, explicitly model it with short, clear examples of both fiction and nonfiction pieces.

Lifesaver Trip #31

http://lesson-plans-materials.suite101.com/article.cfm/visualizing_with_middle_schoolers

This lesson really helps students to "sea" the story come to life!

http://forpd.ucf.edu/strategies/stratvisualization.htm

This trip is a "must sea" for visualization strategies! Rationale and a complete resource list is provided at your fingertips.

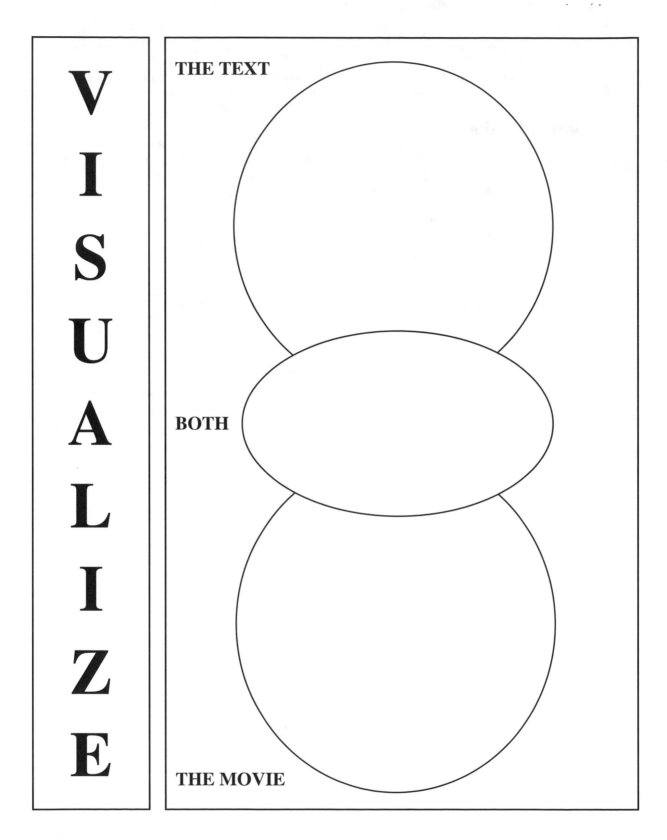

V I S U A L I Z E

THE TEXT

BOTH

THE MOVIE

Lifesaver Tool #31

Literacy Lifesaver #32

Get the Picture?

As you begin to practice visualization strategies, remember that a picture is worth a thousand words. One of the best places to get "practice" pictures is in old magazines. Magazine advertisements are perfect models to use to practice the visualization technique. When you're done with the activity, clean up is a snap—you can simply throw them away!

Lifesaver Tips

- Be sure to preview all magazines you use for cutting and pasting. Obviously, this is critical for primary students, but it's important for secondary students as well. Unfortunately, many magazines tend to include at least one alcohol or tobacco advertisement. You don't want to get a smoke-up from a concerned parent. (By the way, be sure to pull out the classifieds in the back of teen magazines. I learned this the hard way.)

- Your media specialist is a great source for old magazines (especially old *National Geographic* magazines!).

- Lifesaver Tool #32 is a great step-by-step visualization activity for intermediate and secondary students.

- For best results, always model the activity together first before students complete the activity independently.

- When pictures are posted around the room, this activity lends itself nicely to a gallery walk. Provide students with Post-Its so they can leave the artists feedback (positive only allowed!).

- Remind students that drawing ability is not critical—even stick figures can be fun. Help students get the picture when visualizing!

Lifesaver Tweaks

- Because the activity is too hard for younger students, use the "Shut Eye" strategy to describe the picture aloud to elementary students as they visualize the picture you are holding. Then have students open their eyes to see the "real" picture.

- Use the "See and Say" strategy that asks students to describe the differences they saw between the picture in their head and the "real" picture. Discuss possible reasons for their differences.

- Do the flip side of this activity by asking younger students to draw their own pictures and then describe them to you. Go a step further, if time allows, by drawing your own picture on the board as the student gives the description (students love seeing your stick figures).

Lifesaver Trip #32

http://www.howtodrawit.com/

Although drawing ability is not critical, learning to draw can be fun and develop into a life-long hobby. This Web site offers more than fifty free step-by-step drawing lessons. Whether you want to draw a porcupine or a person, this site can help!

Get the Picture in 10 Easy Steps

Visualization Lesson

Suggested Grade Levels: 6–12

Step 1	Distribute magazine pictures to each student. Make sure each picture is clearly numbered.
Step 2	Tell students to describe in writing everything they see in the picture. Remind students that spatial information is critical.
Step 3	Pick up descriptive writing paragraphs and pictures from each student. (For best results, paperclip the paragraph to the picture.)
Step 4	Edit paragraphs and return to authors for revisions. Be sure each paragraph has the corresponding number of the magazine picture clearly labeled at the top of the paper.
Step 5	When paragraphs are completely finished, distribute a paragraph to each student. Be careful not to give a student his or her own paragraph—or the paragraph of a close neighbor!
Step 6	Provide each student with a blank piece of drawing paper, a #2 pencil with eraser, and a set of colored pencils (preferably erasable).
Step 7	Tell students they are now to draw a picture of the descriptive paragraph written by a classmate.
Step 8	Tell students to label their drawing clearly with the appropriate number.
Step 9	Pick up all drawings and paragraphs.
Step 10	Show drawings and original pictures. Compare and contrast the results.

Lifesaver Tool #32

Picture This!

A great way to meet the different learning styles of your students is to have them utilize their visual spatial skills by drawing what they see in their mind's eye. This strategy is most effective when used as a "during" reading activity so students have the opportunity to stop and think during their reading. By pausing and reflecting, readers can more fully comprehend the text or passage.

Lifesaver Tips

- Model this strategy in the media center or in the classroom by using the overhead or SmartBoard. Stop and "talk out loud" while drawing a sketch of the text.

- Specifically teach, model, and practice the difference between a sketch and a detailed drawing.

- Reassure students that they will not be assessed on their "artistic ability" but rather by their ability to verbalize ideas based on their sketches.

- Utilize Lifesaver Tool #33 to provide students with opportunities to practice this strategy with support before expecting independence.

Lifesaver Tweaks

- Be aware that secondary students may be resistant to the idea of drawing (especially with crayons), feeling that they are "too cool" for the activity. Because this reluctance is often caused by a fear of failure, work to provide a risk-free environment and a climate that promotes the idea of risk taking.

- Allow primary students to do more verbalizing before drawing their sketch. Allow for "knee to knee" time to engage in detailed conversations about the book prior to guided practice time.

- Model for several days before expecting younger students to work independently. Students must be encouraged "just to do their best" on drawing their ideas.

- Allow time for volunteers to share their artwork with the whole group. Other, less confident artists may choose not to share with the whole group, electing instead to share their sketches with a partner.

Lifesaver Trip #33

http://teacher.depaul.edu/ResearchBase/Draw2.pdf

Why draw? This site provides all the research behind the power of students using imagery to improve comprehension in their reading. You (and your students) will definitely "sea" the benefits!

Name: _____

Partner's Name: _____

Picture This!

Read the passage on page_____.

1.   Tell your partner the picture you created in your mind as you read or listened to the story.

2.   Listen to your partner's idea.

3.   Re-read the passage. Tell your partner which word/words you found the most vivid or interesting. Which part of the story helped you create your detailed picture in your mind?

4.   Draw your sketch on the back of this sheet! Label it with your key words.

5.   Share your picture with your partner. Compare and contrast the likenesses and differences.

Lifesaver Tool #33

Literacy Lifesaver #34

"Check" Your Vision

This lifesaver simply organizes the visualization strategy by putting it in an easy-to-use checklist format. Enough said!

Lifesaver Tips and Tweaks

- Because Lifesaver #34 is one of the most basic (but also most important) strategies, we combined the tips and tweaks together. As you will see, most of the tips and tweaks apply to all readers, regardless of their "sea" level!

- Older students should regularly use two or three of the visualization strategies on the checklist. Reluctant readers, however, may need modeling and practice to use the visualization strategy effectively.

- Younger students need help using any of the strategies, and they may only learn it with the help of the teacher or media specialist using the "think aloud" strategy and modeling again . . . and again . . . and again!

- Older students can journal what they are seeing as they extend the story; younger students may only be able to describe verbally or predict what might happen next in the story or text.

Lifesaver Trip #34

http://www.lucytravels.com/my-kid-travel-journal-cruises-for-kid.html

Use these printable pages so that students can journal what they "sea" as they read. As students cruise through the book, they can use the printable pages to draw and describe what they read.

Name: _____ Class: _____

Check Your Vision

When I read do I usually …

think of what the character looks like in my head?	
add additional details and scenes to my mental movie—become my own screenwriter (moviemaker) and take the scene further?	
use pictures and images from my own life to help me build BBK (background knowledge) and make connections?	
put myself in the scene—visualize myself being there?	
use all the descriptive words and connect them with my five senses to help me visualize the story?	

Note: You don't always have to use all five "see it" strategies while you read, but a goal should be to use two or three while reading!

Lifesaver Tool #34

Literacy Lifesaver #35

What's Your Point?

Are you looking for strategies to help your students gain a deeper understanding of the text through visualization? This section will point them in the right direction! Students often have difficulty interpreting texts and understanding different points of view. By working with the library media specialist, you can enhance their understanding of this important skill by using the following ideas.

Lifesaver Tips

- Collaborate with the library media specialist to pull a variety of picture books that include different points of view. Folktales and fairy tales often lend themselves well to this unit.

- Divide and conquer! Spend a few weeks using these books as your read-aloud choices, both in the classroom and during library time, to prepare students for this study.

- Begin guided-practice activities by having students draw out a character's name from a hat or basket (Little Red Riding Hood's basket is a favorite of mine). Have students describe the point of view of their characters.

- List ideas on a class chart or SmartBoard. Compare and contrast the various characters' points of view.

- Support students in analyzing their character's point of view (Lifesaver Tool #35).

- Display their work in the library media center as part of an author's celebration.

Lifesaver Tweaks

- Model the strategies with primary students.

- Have secondary students share their creative writings with younger students.

- Provide students opportunities to discuss "real-life" points of view with as many "audience" members as possible. Parents, teachers, and other students often have very different points of view. After discussion, plot how the many different points of view are alike and different.

- Complete the activities in literacy circle groups and during shared reading for time-saving strategies.

- Secondary students can choose to either write or draw about their characters (or both!) using Lifesaver Tool #35.

Lifesaver Trip #35

http://powayusd.sdcoe.k12.ca.us/teachers/dhogan/wkshp /readingcomprehension.htm

Picture some great ways to integrate technology using PowerPoint to promote reading comprehension. Specific examples, including Cinderella, are provided to show different points of view using student drawings and other visualization strategies.

What's Your Point?

Name_____

Title _____

```



```

Main Character's Point of View

```



```

Another Character's Point of View

```



```

Lifesaver Tool #35

Four Square and Seven Words Ago . . .

Whether you're in history class or the media center, vocabulary is critical to literacy success. The best way to build background knowledge is through direct vocabulary instruction. It's no longer enough to give students a list of words and a dictionary; the teacher and/or media specialist must also show the students connections between words and how those words can be used effectively.

Lifesaver Tips and Tweaks

- Use only the top half of Lifesaver Tool #36 for primary students; use both parts for secondary students.

- Use large print dictionaries with both primary and secondary students (even older students love the large print!).

- Refer to dictionary.com with older students.

- Write one vocabulary word on the back of the Four Square form (where it can't be seen) and have students exchange their squares with a friend and guess the correct word.

- Adapt Lifesaver Tool #36 for primary students by completing two or three of the squares with students. Practice and model the four square strategy until even younger students are able to complete more of the squares independently.

Lifesaver Trip #36

http://www.vocabulary.com/top144satwords.html

Do students think you're "square" because you know a lot of words? Don't worry—learn even more at this site, which focuses on the top 144 SAT words! Put your knowledge to the test.

http://pimsleur.english-test.net/vocabularies/elementary-vocabulary-noun-verb-worksheets.html

Find vocabulary worksheets in flashcard format for elementary students here! Your students will improve their vocabulary in a flash!

Four Square Form

WRITE IT!	GUESS IT!

DEFINE IT!	DRAW IT!

ANTONYM:	SYNONYM:

SENTENCE:	BASE WORD:

Lifesaver Tool #36

Literacy Lifesaver #37

Guess What?

Students love guessing games—and so do teachers and librarians when learning is fun! To make learning core vocabulary more interesting and interactive, use these strategies to keep your students guessing! Although this activity is most often done in the classroom, the same tools can be used to teach key vocabulary terms while researching in the media center.

Lifesaver Tips

- Select key vocabulary from the selected story or unit. Don't overlook the opportunity to focus on core vocabulary from social studies, science, or other content-area textbooks.

- Use Lifesaver Tool #37 to have the students predict the meaning of selected vocabulary words.

- Have students listen to the passage from the story (or text) and practice using context clues to determine whether their predictions were correct.

- Ask students to share ideas with partners to confirm or, as the case may be, change their predictions.

- Reveal the "real" definitions of selected vocabulary words after all guessing is complete.

- Assign the words that students missed as vocabulary homework.

Lifesaver Tweaks

- Have students work in groups on the same vocabulary word, rather than individually, if that better fits their needs.

- Consider having a vocabulary challenge with a neighboring class (using the media center for the competition takes the guesswork out of where to stage the competition).

- Create classroom charts of key vocabulary words with which students have difficulty.

- Spiral challenging words back with rereading.

- Discuss the challenge of words with multiple meanings (primary students love *Amelia Bedilia* books!).

Lifesaver Trip #37

http://www.literacymatters.org/content/readandwrite/vocab.htm

This trip contains links to amazing resources and information on teaching vocabulary strategies. "Sea" it for yourself!

Guess What?
Using Context Clues to Learn Vocabulary Words

Name_____

Vocabulary Word_____

My prediction before reading:

My prediction after reading:

_____ Keep it the same!

_____ My partner agreed with me.

_____ My partner and I decided to change my prediction.

My word box of words that helped me make my prediction:

Lifesaver Tool #37

Opposites Attract!

Help your students learn key vocabulary words by using synonyms and antonyms to aid in their comprehension. By diving in to learn what a word is like (synonym) and what it's *not* like (antonym), students will find that opposites attract!

Lifesaver Tips

- Review definitions of synonyms and antonyms as you model examples.

- Select key vocabulary words to target. You don't necessarily have to teach synonyms and antonyms with every word, but even younger students need to have a basic idea of the concept.

- Consider doing this activity in the media center to allow for extra support and resources (class sets of dictionaries!) for researching vocabulary words.

- Utilize Lifesaver Tool #38 during a guided practice activity.

- Have students cut completed blocks apart. Then ask students to join a partner for a game of memory using the antonyms and synonyms. In this game, opposites attract and students have a match if they correctly turn over an antonym and synonym pair.

- Remember that students often learn as much from "non-examples" as they do from specific examples.

Lifesaver Tweaks

- Use Lifesaver Tool #38 on the overhead to model the example prior to having students work in guided practice.

- Utilize the "fish bowl" approach with primary students to demonstrate how to play the memory game and prepare their cards.

- Have students work in cooperative groups on different vocabulary words to raise the difficulty level of the activity as needed.

- Have students save their words in plastic bags and use them at managed independent learning stations or centers as time allows.

Lifesaver Trip #38

http://fen.com/studentactivities/sameDiff/samediff.html

Use this fun and interactive site as a way to model antonyms and synonyms on a presentation screen or SmartBoard. Soon you will see that it will really make a difference!

Opposites Attract!

Synonyms	Antonyms
Vocabulary Word_____	Vocabulary Word_____
Vocabulary Word_____	Vocabulary Word_____
Vocabulary Word_____	Vocabulary Word_____
Vocabulary Word_____	Vocabulary Word_____
Vocabulary Word_____	Vocabulary Word_____

Lifesaver Tool #38

From *100+ Literacy Lifesavers: A Survival Guide for Librarians and Teachers K–12*
by Pamela S. Bacon and Tammy K. Bacon. Westport, CT: Libraries Unlimited. Copyright © 2009.

Literacy Lifesaver #39

Get On a Roll with Vocabulary!

The great thing about a really good strategy is that it can be used over and over again in many different ways. Such is the case with the cubing strategy. As you may recall, we used cubing in Literacy Lifesaver #30 as a BDA (before-during-after) reading strategy. We're using it again here as a vocabulary teaching tool.

Lifesaver Tips and Tweaks

- Use Lifesaver Tool #39 for the basic cubing template.

- The tool also includes sample vocabulary questions for students of all levels.

- Copy the tool onto different colors of paper to help students categorize words. For example, science words could be green and English words red.

- Collaborate with the media specialist and make cubes including key vocabulary terms before starting your research unit in the library.

- Have students put together blank cubes during indoor recess (or after-school detention) so that you always have a supply of cubes ready to go.

- To make cubes reusable, write down a number on each side of the cube. Then use corresponding numbers on a handout for students to refer to (not recommended for younger students).

- Make reusable cubes out of foam for longer durability. If foam is not available, paper and adhesive tape work just fine.

- Provide students with their own cubes for independent work; provide each group with one cube for group work (depending on your lesson objective).

Lifesaver Trip #39

http://forpd.ucf.edu/strategies/stratCubing.html

You will definitely be on a cubing roll once you visit this site. Not only does it explain how to use the cubing strategy in a clear, step-by-step method, it also gives ways to use cubing as an assessment tool.

GET ON A ROLL! CUBING TEMPLATE

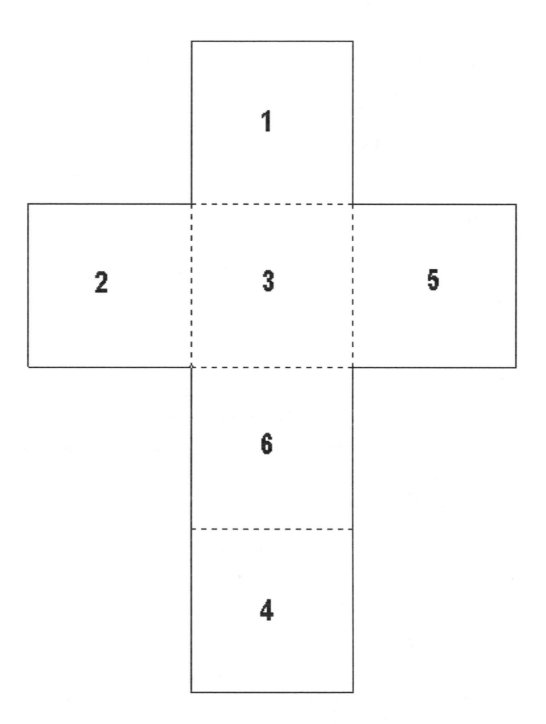

Lifesaver Tool #39

Literacy Lifesaver #40

"Witch/Which" One Do You Mean?

Homonyms (and homophones) can be very confusing to students (what are they, anyway?), yet fun to teach! There are a variety of online quizzes and lists available to share with your students. Lifesaver Tool #40 is an activity in which students create their own homonyms to try and trick their classmates.

Lifesaver Tips and Tweaks

- Add a homonym pair to your word of the day or warm-up activity.

- Create a class chart of popular homonyms for easy reference.

- Collaborate with your media specialist to post library and research-related words.

- Ask your media specialist to pull lists of books that include homonyms.

- Copy ABC charts for students so they can keep homonym pairs listed for easy reference.

- Support primary students by completing the sentences and asking them to circle the homonym/homophone pair (pear?) that correctly completes the sentence.

- Have secondary students make up their own homonym pairs (some real, some imaginary) to try to trick their partners. Example: (scare/scair is not really a homophone couple, but pear/pair is!).

Lifesaver Trip #40

http://www.brainpop.com/english/grammar/antonymssynonymsandhomonyms/

Students and teachers alike will have fun learning about homonyms from a brain pop movie clip and online quiz. "Pop" in to see it!

http://www.cooper.com/alan/homonym.html

You have to "sea" this list to believe it!

"Write" the "Right" Words

Directions:

1. Review the difference between a *homonym* (words that sound the same, are spelled the same, but have different meanings) and a *homophone* (words that sound the same, but have different spellings and meanings).

2. Practice with students using the worksheet below.

3. Need help? Go to http://www.firstschoolyears.com/literacy/word/other/homonyms/homonyms.htm.

Name: _____

Example: The <u>pair</u> of students ate a <u>pear</u>.
Example (make your own!):
List as many homophone pairs as you can.

Lifesaver Tool #40

Lifesaver Notes

_____

_____

_____

_____

_____

_____

_____

_____

_____

_____

_____

_____

_____

_____

_____

_____

_____

_____

_____

_____

_____

Chapter 5

Implementing Literature Circles

Literacy Lifesaver #41

"I've Got a Plan!"

Can you "sea" yourself implementing literature circles with primary students? These very young children need a more structured approach in which the skills and strategies are specifically taught, modeled, and practiced in a whole group first.

Lifesaver Tips

- Collaborate with the media specialist to select a book at the appropriate level with multiple copies for the whole class.

- Work with the media specialist to schedule a booktalk as your literature circle kickoff.

- Once books have been distributed, have students begin reading the book independently or using whisper reading.

- Work with the literature planner as a whole group using the overhead or presentation screen. Note: As a modification, the teacher and librarian can act as a scribe for the students when completing the planner (see Lifesaver Tool #41).

- Use the "fishbowl" approach to demonstrate small-group discussions. This strategy allows the teacher/librarian to demonstrate a technique while other groups gather around to observe (see the glossary). Have students break into small groups for discussion of their literature planners.

- Monitor the groups while taking observational notes of their positive social skills and any behavioral concerns.

- Bring the class back together to create a T-chart of the positive choices and concerns during small group time.

- Plan for specific teaching of any routines/procedures/skills that need to be reinforced before continuing into more independent literature circles.

Lifesaver Tweaks

- Continue to utilize modeling and guided practice with intermediate students.

- Allow for students to read longer chapter books, meeting with the teacher in small groups once or twice a week for book discussions.

- Take time to continue to reinforce positive behaviors at the end of each class period. Although this may seem repetitive, it's critical to keep the students on task and moving forward in cooperative groups.

- With longer books, include several opportunities throughout the readings for summarizing.

- Consider modifying the planner to be used daily, rather than at the end of the book for older students.

- Collaborate with the media specialist to have students take SRC (Scholastic Reading Counts) or AR (Accelerated Reader) quizzes in the media center when they finish reading their literature circle books.

Lifesaver Trip #41

http://home.att.net/~teaching/litcircles.htm

This site includes many tools for creating your own classroom literature circles. It allows you to "dive right in" and get started immediately!

Name_____

Teacher_____

Literature Circle Planner

Book Title: _____

Setting:	
Main Character:	
Main Events: 1. 2. 3. In the circles below, list two "wonderful words" from the story.	

Lifesaver Tool #41

Literacy Lifesaver #42

Sum It Up!

A key skill at the primary level is learning to retell a story with detail and then being able to apply that knowledge when summarizing the story. This literature circle activity provides the necessary tools to help students "sum it up!"

Lifesaver Tips

- Prepare an interactive read-aloud for the classroom or library. During the read, stop to point out important details as they occur.

- Write these details on a large chart or marker board. (If co-teaching with the media specialist, one can read and lead the discussion while the other acts as the recorder.)

- Have students turn and talk to their neighbors to share what they remember. Who were the most important characters?

- Point out any problems as they occur. Tell students that most stories have a problem to solve. What was the problem in the story they just heard? How was it solved?

- After finishing the story, cover the chart and ask students to turn and talk to their neighbors to retell the story.

- Utilize Lifesaver Tool #42 to summarize the story as a whole group. (Note: For very young children, you may want to focus on retelling for several days before summarizing.)

- Put the story summary questions on sentence strips and divide into small groups, allowing one group to focus on one question.

- Monitor the groups and facilitate the discussion.

- Provide group sharing of summary questions.

Lifesaver Tweaks

- Prepare an overhead transparency of Lifesaver Tool #42 for students at the intermediate level.

- Model the tool using a familiar story.

- Allow students to work in groups while one student acts as the scribe to complete the chart.

- Provide small-group sharing to the whole group or allow for the recorder to jigsaw to other groups. Note: Before using this strategy, be sure to model this cooperative group activity.

Lifesaver Trip #42

http://www.literaturecircles.com/

This site provides teachers and librarians the opportunity to get advice and share ideas with others in the trenches who are already implementing literature circles.

Name_____

Date _____

Literature Circle Observational Notes

Book Title: _____

Student can retell most of the story in order.

     5   **4**   **3**   **2**   **1**

Student can retell most of the story in order.

     5   **4**   **3**   **2**   **1**

Student can retell most of the story in order.

     5   **4**   **3**   **2**   **1**

Teacher Observations: (example: Student responds with higher-level thinking. Student can describe the problem and solutions in the story.)

Lifesaver Tool #42

Literacy Lifesaver #43

Ask Me Anything!

At first, it seems primary students will never learn the difference between a question and a comment. (Attend any convocation during the question-and-answer session to confirm this!) Once they have learned what a good question is—and how to answer specific questions during and after reading—it's time to teach them how to create questions.

Lifesaver Tips

- Begin with a review of the difference between a statement and a question.

- Point out specific examples of each in big books and shared readings.

- Have them work in small groups to find examples of each. (Very young students can place bookmarks or sticky notes on their pages, and older students can write the examples.)

- Use Lifesaver Tool #43 as a whole-group guided practice activity.

- Work with the media specialist to divide the class into two groups. Have each group create questions, with the adults acting as scribes.

- Switch question sheets and see whether each group can answer the other's questions.

- Review the skill in future lessons by having students divide into small groups with a common book and create one question from Lifesaver Tool #43.

- Have one student act as a scribe and complete the question sheet when students are able to work independently on the skill.

Lifesaver Tweaks

- Have intermediate students complete Lifesaver Tool #43 in small groups using the same book or different books.

- Consider having older students complete the question sheet independently as part of their self-selected or independent reading time.

- Continue to model the questioning process by "talking out loud" as you reflect over read-aloud stories.

- Consider having older students pair with younger students to act as scribes as students learn how to ask good questions.

Lifesaver Trip #43

http://eduscapes.com/ladders/themes/circles.htm

This site provides a wealth of information including a primary link with time lines, book suggestions, and literature circle structures specific to first grade.

Name _____

Date _____

Ask Me Anything!

Book Title: _____

Who were the main characters? **Who** was YOUR favorite?
What might happen next?
When did the story take place?
Why did _____? Give your opinion.
How would YOU solve the problem in the story?

Lifesaver Tool #43

Word Search!

Primary students love to do word search puzzles! This activity teaches students to learn to notice "wonderful words" in their stories. Before children can use vivid words in their writing, they need to have many experiences listening to powerful stories and reading great books. Use the tool in this section to help students learn to have fun searching for wonderful words.

Lifesaver Tips

- Stop often during read-aloud time to point out examples of "wonderful words."

- Discuss what makes the word wonderful (i.e., What makes a word "special?").

- Utilize author studies as a way to share powerful language with students while learning about the author's style.

- Collaborate with the media specialist to develop several author collections for use in literature circles.

- Co-plan lessons using each of your favorite picture books that include wonderful words to bring the story to life.

- Use sticky notes to highlight wonderful words, and encourage students to notice words as they listen to stories or read independently.

- Divide into small groups while co-teaching with the media specialist. Have students use Lifesaver Tool #44 to list vivid words. (Younger students can place Post-It notes on their favorite words.)

- Bring the class back together for sharing. Create a class chart of wonderful words.

- Encourage students to add to the chart as they continue their independent word searches.

Lifesaver Tweaks

- Intermediate students can take this activity a step further by categorizing words.

- Have students log interesting words in their reader's notebooks by listing the story, word, and page number.

- Use Lifesaver Tool #44 during literature circles while one student acts as the recorder of wonderful words.

- Create classroom posters for different types of words; include students in creating the categories. What words are interesting . . . hard . . . weird?

- Encourage students to use the author's language in their writing. Post their samples to reinforce the application of the "wonderful word" strategy.

- Model dictionary use to locate word meanings for any unfamiliar words. This could also be a role for one of the group members.

Lifesaver Trip #44

http://www.litcircles.org

This comprehensive Web site includes examples for all grade levels. It is a "must-visit" site for any teacher or librarian implementing literature circles!

Name_____

Teacher_____

"Word Search"

Book Title: _____

Pages Read: _____

```
                        ┌──────────────────┐
                        │  Wonderful Words  │
                        └──────────────────┘
              ┌──────────────────┼──────────────────┐
     ┌────────────────┐  ┌────────────────┐  ┌────────────────┐
     │   Interesting  │  │     Unique     │  │      Vivid     │
     │                │  │   or unusual   │  │                │
     └────────────────┘  └────────────────┘  └────────────────┘
```

In the spaces below, search for three wonderful words. List the word, the page number, and check yes or no if you know the meaning of the word.

Word _____

Page # _____

I know what this word means.   Yes   or   No

Word _____

Page # _____

I know what this word means.   Yes   or   No

Word _____

Page # _____

I know what this word means.   Yes   or   No

Lifesaver Tool #44

From *100+ Literacy Lifesavers: A Survival Guide for Librarians and Teachers K–12* by Pamela S. Bacon and Tammy K. Bacon. Westport, CT: Libraries Unlimited. Copyright © 2009.

Literacy Lifesaver #45

Win, Lose, or Draw!

It is important for primary students to remember the importance of creating pictures in their minds as they read. That keeps them from "losing" their comprehension. Use this activity to "draw" students out and keep them moving forward in their literacy learning.

Lifesaver Tips

- Model the "stop and think" procedure during interactive read-aloud activities to help students pause to visualize a picture in their mind of what is happening in the story.

- Use a large chart during co-teaching to allow for the teacher or librarian to sketch the ideas as they occur.

- Teach students the difference between "drawing with details" and "sketching" main ideas.

- Use Lifesaver Tool #45 to model the process on the overhead while talking out loud about the picture.

- Divide students into small groups to discuss a specific part of the story and what pictures they might sketch.

- Provide sharing time and discuss what makes a good sketch. (If time allows, sketches can be colored and completed for display in the media center.)

Lifesaver Tweaks

- Remind intermediate students about the difference between sketching and drawing; some students will spend what may seem like forever on their masterpieces.

- Consider having older students fold their blank papers into four squares to sketch more than one idea per page.

- Divide students into several roles while meeting in literature circles for the same (or different) books.

- Show picture books during author studies to show how pictures carry meaning.

- Remind older students that illustrations can include a diagram, cartoon, or chart.

Lifesaver Trip # 45

http://www.education-world.com/a_curr/curr259.shtml

This site describes in detail how to get started with literature circles. Specific roles, things to consider, and grouping are all covered. Here is everything you need to "launch" your program!

Win, Lose, or Draw!

Book Title: _____

Page: _____

Make a sketch of the most important event in your story.

In the space below, write at least two sentences that tell what your picture is mostly about.

_____

_____

_____

_____

Lifesaver Tool #45

Plan on It!

The biggest key to success—and the biggest challenge—when implementing literature circles is planning. Every second needs to be thought-out and planned. Problems start when students have too much (or any!) free time. Therefore, it's time to get a plan!

Lifesaver Tips

- Copy the Literature Circle Planner and Reading Calendar (Lifesaver Tool #46) front-to-back on 11 x 14 paper to make a nice planning booklet for students.

- Use different colors of paper for different groups (example: *The Great Gatsby*—green and *Of Mice and Men*—yellow). Although not mandatory, color-coding is a nice organizational technique and visual cue to help with paperwork management.

- Divide the planner into user-friendly sections as follows (tweak as needed to make it work for you):

    Page 1: Cover (includes title, author, a place for illustration, and identification information)

    Page 2: Reading Goal (plan for number of pages to read per day) and reading calendar/schedule, and procedural notes

    Page 3: Roles (assignments for each literature circle member) and responsibilities

    Page 4: Reflections (space to respond to assigned journal prompts)

- Distribute new planners weekly.

- Provide the media specialist with a copy of your planner so that he or she can be prepared to assist students when visiting the media center to check out or renew books.

- Ask the media specialist to provide journal prompts to tie in key media center literacy skills during your literature circle unit.

Lifesaver Tweaks

- This activity could easily be adapted for intermediate students. Unlike the secondary students who can handle changes in structure (usually!), intermediate students might do better with assigned roles that do not rotate. This added structure will help intermediate students be more successful.

- Keep planners in the classroom or library for intermediate students. Older students should take their planners home to log assigned reading or write additional journal topics.

- Add three to five "generic" journal choices to the planner for intermediate students. Older students can refer to an additional handout for journal prompts.

- Shorten required journal length to a minimum of three sentences for intermediate students if needed (based on time restrictions and/or ability).

Lifesaver Trip #46

http://www.studyguide.org/lit_circles_high_school.htm

This site is your one-stop shop for literature circles. Everything is included, from setting up, to implementing, to evaluating literature circles. It's a great place to get your feet wet—dive in!

LITERATURE CIRCLE PLANNER

_____

TITLE OF NOVEL

_____

AUTHOR OF NOVEL

Draw a picture of the front of your book above.

Name_____

Class Period_____

Group Name_____

Lifesaver Tool #46

Reading Calendar

Title of Book_____ Number of Pages_____

Number of Days to Read_____

<u>Directions:</u> In the calendar below, plan the page numbers you intend to read for each day. Write the pages in pencil in case your plans change and pages need to be adjusted.

MONDAY	TUESDAY	WEDNESDAY	THURSDAY	FRIDAY	GOAL MET ☺

READING ROLES:

Discussion Director_____

Line Leader_____

Connection Collector_____

Picture Person_____

Lifesaver Tool #46

Directions: Choose your own topic to write about in the space below, or write on the assigned topic.

DAILY JOURNAL
Date: _____
Date: _____
Date: _____
Date: _____
Date: _____

Lifesaver Tool #46

DAILY DRAWING	MONDAY
TUESDAY	WEDNESDAY
THURSDAY	FRIDAY

Lifesaver Tool #46

Literacy Lifesaver #47

Do You Use That Line Often?

This activity encourages students to dive into their literature circle novels and analyze their favorite (or least favorite) lines. One of the biggest hurdles for students is reading comprehension, which obviously includes understanding and analyzing what they read. By breaking the text down into meaningful lines, you'll be able to assess whether they understand the key parts of what they are reading.

Lifesaver Tips

- Use the top of Lifesaver Tool #47 daily for students to record both their favorite lines (referred to as "Golden Lines") and rationales as to why those particular lines were chosen. Note: Golden lines are lines that stand out more than others because they contain imagery, figurative language, foreshadowing, irony, humor, are beautifully written, or relate to you in some way.

- Use the bottom half of the tool weekly for students to self-reflect on their progress and preparation for that time period.

- Use the media center on a weekly basis. The media specialist can be a huge support to you in modeling additional "golden lines" or providing evaluative feedback on literature circle groups.

- Ask students to rate themselves on the self-evaluation rubric with a yellow highlighter. When you (or the media specialist) evaluate, use a highlighter of a different color. This quick and easy evaluation strategy saves valuable time (and paper!).

Lifesaver Tweaks

- Tell intermediate students to turn in daily one "golden lines" paper per group (instead of one per person). Intermediate students will need additional time to complete the activity and engage in quality group discussion. The general rule is that the more detailed the discussion, the higher the quality of response.

- Focus on only one of the following self-evaluation topics weekly: reading, writing, discussion, listening, preparation. By focusing on each skill separately (while modeling and practicing), students will better adapt to the more unstructured literature circle format.

- Stay on skills longer if necessary. For example, middle school students often need additional focus on listening and preparation; older students are more able to multitask and meet multiple skills simultaneously (depending on ability and maturity).

Lifesaver Trip #47

http://www.funtrivia.com/en/Literature/Famous-First-Lines-15010.html

This amazing site offers trivia quizzes that focus on famous lines of novels. For example, do you know what famous work includes the line, "Call me Ishmael"? You'll have to go to the site to get the answer!

What's Your Line?

Directions: Write down your favorite ("golden") line and the page number where it is found in the table below.

Day	Golden Line	Page
M		
T		
W		
Th		
F		

Get Your Group "In Line!"

Directions: Write down important notes from your group discussion daily.

Day	Discussion Notes	Score (out of 10)
M		
T		
W		
Th		
F		

Lifesaver Tool #47

Anecdote Notes:
Evaluating Literature
Circle Discussion

When the students turn in work, it's usually easy (but time-consuming!) to evaluate their progress. What's not so easy is to evaluate literature discussions. Certainly, the noise level in the room is one easy-to-recognize indicator of engaged discussion. Another way is by asking the right anecdotal focus questions. Are you prepared?

Lifesaver Tips

1. Is the student engaged in the discussion? Does body language indicate engagement?

2. Does the student participate verbally in the group discussion?

3. Does the student use textual support to support his or her opinions and ideas?

4. Does the student use new vocabulary terms in discussion?

5. Does the student connect the text to his or her life, world, other texts?

6. Does the student reference literary devices (metaphors, similes, tone) in his or her discussion?

7. Does the student use literary elements in his or her discussion (plot, setting, theme character, conflict)?

8. Does the student listen to others' comments and build on that discussion?

Note: Lifesaver Tool #48 provides a space to record anecdotal notes and observational assessments.

Lifesaver Tweaks

- Most of the previous questions can be asked of intermediate students.

- Question #6 (which asks for literary devices and higher-level analysis) may need to be deleted or modified.

- Listening skills (Question #8) are especially critical at the intermediate level.

- Provide a copy of these questions prior to dividing into literature circle groups in the media center.

- Complete a simple T-chart together with intermediate students prior to starting literature circles. Title the T-Chart "Talk about Discussion." On the left side, discuss what good discussion looks like (i.e., desks close together). On the right side, discuss what good discussion sounds like (i.e., "What do you think?," What's your opinion?").

Lifesaver Trip #48

http://www.litcircles.org/Discussion/format.html

This site includes specific information on discussion strategies for secondary students. In addition, sample handouts are included for you to "sea!"

Student_____ Period_____

Literature Circle Group_____

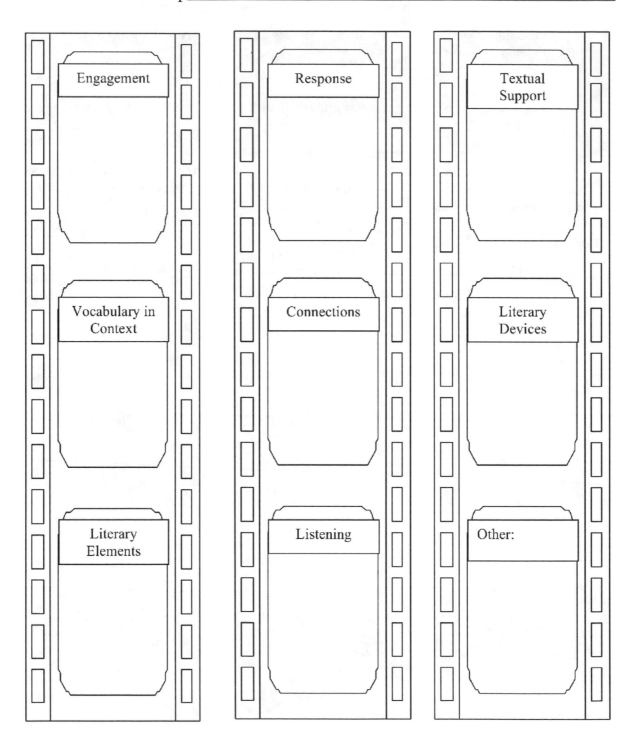

That "Sums" It Up!

Even though summarizing is explicitly taught in the earlier grade levels, it continues to be an important skill for secondary students. When comprehending increasingly difficult texts, they need to practice summarizing frequently during their independent reading. By spiraling this skill and coaching students on the components of a good summary, they will have it "summed" up in no time!

Lifesaver Tips

- Model how to create statements that convey "the gist" of the story.

- Show students how to record key points and the main highlight of the story in their reader's notebooks.

- Utilize the "talk out loud" strategy to model how to summarize a read-aloud (the teacher or library media specialist talks out loud to help students learn a skill; similar to the "think out loud" strategy).

- Provide opportunities to practice the skill verbally, prior to having a guided practice with Lifesaver Tool #49.

- After the students demonstrate mastery of the skill, assign Lifesaver Tool #49 to be done independently in small groups.

- Monitor the groups and take observational notes (preferably with the media specialist assisting).

Lifesaver Tweaks

- Provide additional guided practice of Lifesaver Tool #49 with intermediate students; they may find it difficult to get their ideas down in writing.

- Consider having students work in pairs prior to small groups.

- Use the same book for the first practice of summarizing with literature circles.

- Explicitly teach the difference between retelling a story and telling what the story is "mostly about."

Lifesaver Trip #49

http://litsite.alaska.edu/workbooks/circlereading.html

Take a trip to Alaska to view this wonderful site! It includes everything from role ideas to modified worksheets to include different learning needs. These great ideas won't leave you "on thin ice" with your students!

Name _____

Teacher/Period _____

Literature Circle Group _____

Book Title _____

Assigned pages _____ to _____

Your task today is to prepare a story summary of today's reading. It is your task to write a quick one- to two-minute statement that includes the key points and main events of your assignment. Write your summary in the space below and turn it in at the end of your literature circle meeting.

Summary:

_____

_____

_____

_____

_____

_____

_____

_____

_____

_____

Lifesaver Tool #49

Literacy Lifesaver #50

Talk about Discussion!

Talking is a skill that you may think students have already mastered. (How many times have you said "Shhh!" in the library?) However, teaching students to engage in quality, deeper-level discussions is a subject worth talking about!

Lifesaver Tips

- Model the "think aloud" strategy when starting to teach discussion strategies.

- Use the fishbowl technique so that students can see a group in action that is engaged in higher-level discussion. This strategy allows the teacher/librarian to demonstrate higher-level thinking and discussion while other groups gather around to observe (see the glossary).

- Practice, practice, practice! Don't get discouraged—it may take some time, but you will start to see better discussions taking place if you wait it out.

- Use a timer to add more structure. Teach students that when the timer goes off, so do their voices!

- Create a signal (or use the timer again) to get students to pause when you want to interrupt their discussions to make some key points.

- Lifesaver Tool #50 provides a place to record questions prior to discussion for smoother sailing!

Lifesaver Tweaks

- Use the same tips for intermediate students—just be prepared to take additional time for modeling, "fish-bowling," and practicing before you begin to see discussion growth.

- Be patient!

- Take pictures of students engaging in quality language. Analyze the pictures with your students. What do quality discussions look like? Who (in the picture) is modeling good body language and listening skills?

Lifesaver Trip #50

http://www.sedl.org/afterschool/toolkits/literacy/pr_book_groups.html

This site includes great ideas for literacy circles, as well as suggestions for motivating students through an online discussion of their books. Check this out for a great technology link!

Name _____

Teacher/Period _____

Literature Circle Group _____

Book Title _____

Assigned pages: _____ to _____

Your task today is to develop a list of at least six questions that your group will discuss to get the most out of this section of the story. Consider your own thoughts, feelings, and ideas as you read. Try to think of interesting questions that go beyond yes or no answers.

Sample questions:

How are your feelings like the character's thoughts and feelings?
Have you had some of the experiences similar to those of the main character?
Ask for predictions—what might happen next in the story?
How do you think the problem will be resolved in the story?

Discussion Leader Questions:

1. _____
   _____

2. _____
   _____

3. _____
   _____

4. _____
   _____

5. _____
   _____

6. _____
   _____

Lifesaver Tool #50

Lifesaver Notes

_____

_____

_____

_____

_____

_____

_____

_____

_____

_____

_____

_____

_____

_____

_____

_____

_____

_____

_____

_____

_____

Lifesaver Notes

_____

_____

_____

_____

_____

_____

_____

_____

_____

_____

_____

_____

_____

_____

_____

_____

_____

_____

_____

_____

Chapter 6

Visiting Authors and Author's Purpose

Literacy Lifesaver #51

Visiting Authors—"Check" Them Out!

Author visits are truly one of the most rewarding ways to enhance literacy instruction. In addition to promoting reading, a strength of author visits is the focus on writing and the ability to "dive" deeper into the writing craft. This section focuses on grade-level-specific titles and authors; therefore, no specific tweaks are listed. However, as always, each school will want to tweak the lifesaver tools and information to meet the needs of their specific students and/or audiences. Author visits aren't hard to arrange, but can be time-consuming for the hosting media specialist. Many authors have their own checklists for specific items they need, but our checklists will divide the tasks for a collaborative program. Anchors and authors away!

Lifesaver Tips

- Determine who will be the primary contact for your author.

- Create, plan, and organize a team to ensure the success of your visiting author program.

- Don't forget to include PTO members and parent volunteers as part of the planning process.

- Write grants to help fund visiting authors, who can be costly.

- Collaborate with other media specialists in the district and in other local schools to help cut costs.

- Send the date to the principal as soon as it is established.

- Before you set the date, check the master schedule to make sure your author visit doesn't conflict with another major school event.

- Refer to Lifesaver Tool #51 for a detailed, task-specific visiting author checklist.

Lifesaver Trip #51

http://www.fortbend.k12.tx.us/library/docs/Author%20Handbook%20v02.pdf

This is your one-stop shop for author visits! Look no further—Great job, Fort Wayne!

Visiting Author Planning Checklist

Author: _____

Date of Visit: _____

Task List   **Assigned to**

_____ Overall event coordination

_____ Securing date of event with author

_____ Transportation arrangements

_____ Hotel/lodging

_____ Presentation area: Seating arrangements, audiovisual

_____ Book ordering for classrooms/library

_____ Book sales before, during, and after event

_____ Book signing arrangements

_____ Presentation schedule

_____ Author meals, snacks, and drinks

_____ Student materials for visit

_____ Payments to author

_____ Public relations/promotions

_____ Directions and informational packet sent to author

_____ Other:

Lifesaver Tool #51

From *100+ Literacy Lifesavers: A Survival Guide for Librarians and Teachers K–12*
by Pamela S. Bacon and Tammy K. Bacon. Westport, CT: Libraries Unlimited. Copyright © 2009.

Literacy Lifesaver #52

View Visiting Authors!

This Literacy Lifesaver is a step-by-step walk through the visiting authors.com site. Just getting started, or just thinking about hosting a children's book author and/or illustrator? This is the place for you! You can "picture" a great author visit, can't you?

Lifesaver Tips

- Gather information here on 16 different children's authors and illustrators (see Lifesaver Trip#51).

- Begin author studies with your students. Study authors' works during literature circles.

- The media specialist can assign different authors to different classrooms for review.

- After the initial author study, students can use Lifesaver Tool #52 to jigsaw the information and presentations for other classes.

- Use live announcements to get out information regarding the process.

- Hold a schoolwide vote using the media center as a polling place.

- Celebrate the winning author and begin planning. A link to help you plan a successful author visit is found in Lifesaver Trip #52.

Lifesaver Trip #52

http://www.visitingauthors.com/

This link includes information on everything from planning a successful visit to book ordering information, as well as printable author's pages. "Sea" it for yourself!

Name _____

Teacher _____

Date _____

Introducing the Author

My author is _____.

Biographical information:

Three books that I would like to read:

Three interesting facts about this author:

This is my favorite line from the book _____:

Lifesaver Tool #52

Explore Planet Esme!

Esme Raji Codell is one of a kind. A self-proclaimed "readiologist," Esme has written wonderfully creative children's books. The zany author has also written a new book, *How to Get Your Child to Love Reading* (Algonguin, 2003), written specifically for a parent audience. This wildly exciting author owns her own bookroom in Chicago, Illinois, geared toward parents and teachers, but the author admits children can visit too!

Lifesaver Tips

- Read aloud every chance you get. Esme refers to reading aloud as "the great equalizer," which allows all children equal access to the magic within books.

- Remind teachers of the value of read-alouds.

- Ensure that all parents, especially hard-to-reach and high-poverty parents, are invited and encouraged to attend a visiting author event.

- Work to acquire funds for all parents who attend to receive copies of *How to Get Your Child to Love Reading*. Local businesses could use this financial gift as a tax write-off and perform a valuable community service.

- Collaborate, promote, and prepare Esme's reading-related activities before hosting this famous author. Activities could be completed prior to the author visit or after for a culminating event.

- Utilize Esme's Book a Day Blog with teachers to encourage more great classroom read-alouds.

- Include read alouds in your newsletter.

- Show the video clip prior to the author visit to encourage students to visit this purple-haired wonder (warning: hair color may change prior to visit!).

- Lifesaver Tool #53 provides a handy spot to list your favorite picture books to share with students—or to order!

Lifesaver Trip #53

http://www.planetesme.com/

This author, and this site, are truly out of this world! Visit often!

Name_____

Date/Year_____

"Picture Perfect" Book List

Keep this page handy to list your favorite picture books to share with teachers and staff for easy reference. Pamela S. Bacon and Tammy K. Bacon. Westport, CT: Libraries Unlimited. Copyright © 2009.

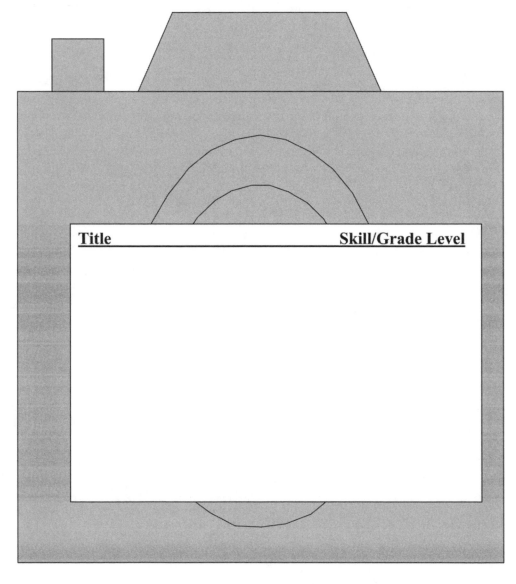

Title	Skill/Grade Level

Lifesaver Tool #53

Literacy Lifesaver #54

It's a Mystery!

Meet Michele Torrey—just "in case" you are planning an upcoming author visit!

Michele Torrey is an accomplished author of a series of science mysteries for students in Grades 3–5. In addition, she has written several historical fiction books that will appeal to students at the middle school level. Her Web site provides students with great biographical information so that, when this visiting author comes, she "won't be a mystery!"

Lifesaver Tips

- Order an adequate number of books for literature circles and read-alouds in classrooms.

- Specifically teach the genre of historical fiction and mysteries in library lessons to help support students as they begin reading this new genre.

- Include cross-curricular study as appropriate for the text.

- Encourage students to do library research to support background knowledge of the area of study.

- Create character maps of the main characters so that students feel as if they know them prior to hosting the author visit.

- Utilize Literacy Lifesaver #54 as you read the science mysteries to focus on the suspects and look for clues.

- Use the "My Books" link from Lifesaver Trip #54 to introduce Torrey's books to students and assist them in selecting their book to read prior to the visit.

Lifesaver Trip #54

http://www.micheletorrey.com/index.htm

"Sea" Torrey's Stories here!

Name_____

Teacher_____

"It's a Mystery"

Character	Character Traits	Incriminating Evidence (list page numbers)
1.		
2.		
3.		
4.		

Predict how you think the mystery will be solved.

Lifesaver Tool #54

Author Visits—They're "Virtually Possible"!

If your school is limited on time or money—or both—you can collaborate with teachers to create a unit of study based on a virtual field trip. By using the author's Web site and a presentation screen, students can get "up close and personal" with the author in the comfort of their own classroom, library, or computer lab.

Lifesaver Tips

- Collaborate with teachers to determine which author study they would like to focus on for their "visit."

- "Surf" the available Web sites to ensure that they are working and provide sufficient information for your unit.

- As always with technology, have a backup plan ready!

- Select which books students will be reading or writing about during the unit.

- Consider utilizing journals for response logs and for brainstorming questions that students have about the author. Literacy Lifesaver #55 provides students with some examples of questions and space to write their own which may be done individually, or in small groups. With very young students, this may be done on a chart as a shared writing that could be mailed to the author.

- Send the author questions from your students by snail mail or to his or her e-mail contact information from the Web site. This is a great "pre-visit" activity. Students could also send questions after the "visit" and await a "real" response.

- Encourage other classrooms to select different authors and then hold an "Authors Fair" at the culmination of the unit.

- Use video clips available on many author's Web sites as part of the kickoff to the unit to capture the audience from the start.

- Create graphic organizers and charts to compare and contrast the authors' works.

- Stop and share the "author's language" during read-alouds to help students notice key elements of the writings.

Lifesaver Trip #55

http://www.janbrett.com/

Visit Jan Brett's Web site for beautiful illustrations from her books. Students will get a close-up introduction to her wonderful characters as well as activity downloads to extend their learning.

http://www.eric-carle.com/home.html

Although Eric Carle states that he is cutting down on author visits because of his "semi-retirement," his Web site includes a wealth of information including video clips that will entice students and teachers alike.

Name_____

Teacher_____

Below are some questions that we might consider asking our author. Circle your favorites and write your own in the space that follows.

- How did you create your characters?
- How long did it take you to write_____?
- Which book is your favorite?
- Would you change any of your books if you could?

. . . .

Write your questions here:

Literacy Lifesaver #55

Sharon Draper: This Author Is "Booked!"

Walk into any middle school or high school, say the name "Sharon Draper," and students will start rambling off book titles written by this beloved author, writer, poet, and speaker. Draper, who has won numerous awards for her books, is perhaps best known at the secondary level for her Hazelwood trilogy, consisting of *Tears of a Tiger*, *Forged by Fire,* and *Darkness before Dawn*. Less well known, however, is her new series for younger children, *Ziggy & the Black Dinosaurs*. Any school would be delighted to hear this author (I've heard her, and she's awesome!)—if they're lucky enough to get her. The author is very selective about which schools she will visit and has certain requirements that must be met before she will agree to come. If you're patient and persistent, however, (this busy author schedules her own visits), the wait will be well worth it!

Lifesaver Tips

- Read Sharon Draper's personal guidelines (http://sharondraper.com/guidelines.pdf) before scheduling an author visit. Unlike some authors, who are glad to visit any school willing to pay the presentation costs and travel fees, Draper is very selective in the schools she chooses to visit. She will only attend schools where all of the students have read at least one of her books, and prefers the students (and staff) to have read more than one. Between teaching, writing, and author visits, this author is truly "booked!"

- Because Draper's schedule is normally "booked" up to a year (or more) ahead of time, the author suggests using her media kit in the meantime. The media kit (some are available free of charge or at highly reduced rates) includes a life-sized author cutout, CDs, DVDs, bookmarks and other author promotional materials.

- Use the media kit before Draper's visit as part of an author study. You might even dress the Draper cutouts in your own school colors to create an author mascot!

- Visit Draper virtually at her homepage (see Lifesaver Trip #56) to view free author talks.

- Print and distribute free literature guides to students and teachers prior to the author visit.

- To generate interest in the author visit, create a "Draper Discussion" trivia game and ask students questions about Draper on the daily announcements. Students can go to Draper's biography (see Lifesaver Trip #56) to answer questions.

- Write the author! Although she can't promise to answer every letter, she does answer many. Her Web site includes dozens of author letters that were sent to her. These letters can be used to brainstorm types of questions to ask the author prior to writing individual letters. Be sure to visit the "Homework Helper" section of her homepage to make sure that your students' questions haven't already been asked—and answered!

- Lifesaver Tool #56 is a graphic organizer to use with her Hazelwood High Trilogy—and a great way to review before the author visit!

Lifesaver Tweaks

- Elementary students would love to hear the author speak about her new series, Ziggy and the Black Dinosaurs! Characters answer silly questions online and coloring pages are also available.

- Sponsor a coloring page contest prior to the author visit to encourage young artists and writers!

Lifesaver Trip #56

http://www.sharondraper.com/

Everything you need for a great Draper author visit can found here. You can view sample author talks and booktalks, discover biographical information, order books at a discount, or find out about free or reduced media kits. Dive in, and don't forget a snack—you'll be here awhile!

Name_____

Teacher_____ Period_____

Graphic Organizer: Draper Paper

<u>Directions:</u> Compare and contrast the three books in the Hazelwood High trilogy: *Tears of a Tiger, Darkness before Dawn,* and *Forged by Fire.*

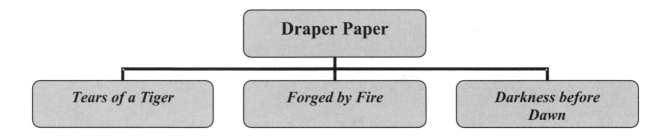

Lifesaver Tool #56

Literacy Lifesaver #57

Virtual Visit to Billy Shakespeare Land!

If you're reading this book, it is most likely that you are a "Hamburger-a-gogo" fan (i.e., from the United States). It is possible, however, that you're reading this in "Billy Shakespeare" land (where one-of-a-kind author Louise Rennison resides). This virtual visiting author visit will allow your students to get up close and personal with Georgia Nicholson (Rennison's fabitty fab main character). You'll also meet other characters, like Angus (a very strange boy kitty-kat) and all kinds of human boys whom Georgia obsesses over. Written in diary form, your readers will all flock to the shelves to find out all about Georgia's latest snogging (i.e., kissing) adventures. Pucker up!

Lifesaver Tips

- Do not give students detentions for disruptive laughter. This book is laugh-out-loud hilarious!

- Host a virtual visit night at the library. Take your students (maybe book club members!) to "Billy Shakespeare" land.

- Allow time to sign up for the fabbity fab fan club and go on message boards.

- Remind students that there will be no snogging allowed!

- Meet the Ace Gang up close and personal. The students will feel like their chums in no time!

- View the Video Interviews with Author Louise Rennison. The author shares biographical information and provides clips of the latest and greatest on her upcoming movie, *Angus, Thongs & Full Frontal Snogging!*

- Host a contest! Tell students to visit the Georgia Glossary and see who can stay in character and talk like Georgia all night!

- Host a sleepover and stay up all night reading Rennison's latest book in the series, *Love Is a Many Trousered Thing*.

- Lifesaver Tool #57 is a place to keep track of Georgia, Angus, and their misadventures!

Lifesaver Trip #57

http://www.georgianicolson.com

Hey, best mates! Travel to "Billy Shakespeare" land and plan to laugh out loud! Tee hee hee! Say hi to Angus while you're there!

Name_____

Teacher_____ Period_____

"Fabbity-Fab" Favorites by Georgia Nicolson

Title: *Angus, Thongs and Full-Frontal Snogging*
Comments:

_____
_____
_____
_____
_____

Title: *It's OK, I'm Wearing Really Big Knickers*
Comments:

_____
_____
_____
_____
_____

Title: *Knocked Out by My Nunga-Nungas*
Comments:

_____
_____
_____
_____
_____

Title: *Dancing in My Nuddy-Pants*
Comments:

_____
_____
_____
_____
_____

Lifesaver Tool #57

Title: . . . *And That's When It Fell Off in My Hand*
Comments:

_____

_____

_____

_____

_____

Title: *Then He Ate My Boy Entrancers*
Comments:

_____

_____

_____

_____

_____

Title: . . . *Startled by His Furry Shorts!*
Comments:

_____

_____

_____

_____

_____

Title: *Luuurve Is a Many Trousered Thing*
Comments:

_____

_____

_____

_____

_____

Lifesaver Tool #57

Whose House? Keesha's House!

Whose House? Keesha's House! That's what students will be saying after the author visit by Helen Frost! Frost is an Indiana native and accomplished writer of books for children and adolescents. Frost's most popular book, *Keesha's House*, is a verse novel and will soon be made into a movie. The author has also written a book for educators on teaching writing. In addition to having her visit your students, consider linking with this author for a professional development opportunity to motivate teachers in the area of writing.

Lifesaver Tips

- Include the book *Keesha's House* as a kickoff to this author project. Ensure that multiple copies are available for classroom sets or read-alouds. Because of the high interest level and the teen issues it considers, this book may end up at students' houses!

- Collaborate with teachers on studying the unique genre of verse novels. Verse novels are a great chance to read-aloud snippets of popular books.

- Encourage students to use journals and experiment with Frost's format of writing.

- Create questions for the author as a class prior to the visit. Vote for favorites to include in the presentation.

- Encourage the school counselor to use some of Frost's works, which include students who have experienced violence and family problems.

- Include Frost's work in collaborative cross-curricular units such as *Monarch and Milkweed,* which is a lyrical, nonfiction work.

- Visit Frost's Web site link for teaching ideas that connect to her books (see Lifesaver Tool #58 for one example).

- Include Frost's plays as part of Reader's Theatre or a production, if time allows.

Lifesaver Trip #58

http://www.helenfrost.net/index.php

Frost's Web site contains specific information on her novels, plays, and anthologies. In addition, this award-winning author has several unique links to the site including the movie link to *Keesha's House.* Students will also enjoy visiting the author's Facebook page, which was recently added to the site!

Keesha's House

Directions: Choose any three characters from the book. List their name and three characteristics of that person in the spaces below. List the page number and reason or "proof" from the book for your choice.

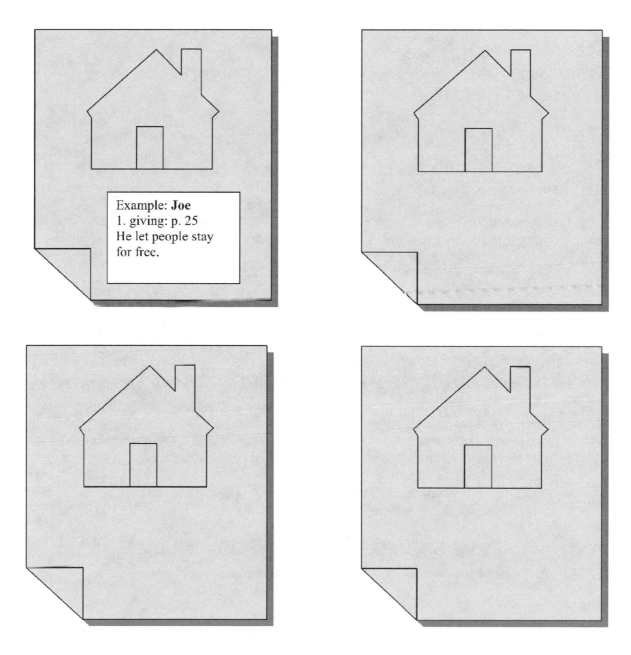

Example: **Joe**
1. giving: p. 25
He let people stay for free.

Lifesaver Tool #58

Gordan Korman: "Dive" into Great Books!

Perhaps best known for his Dive series (the most recent book in the series is *The Danger*; Scholastic, 2003), author Gordan Korman is a great visiting author. His trademark humor and lively presentation makes this author a must-have at your school. Not only does he give quality booktalks about his 50+ published books, he is also a great writing workshop speaker who motivates young authors (he wrote his first book when he was only 12, and Scholastic published it when he was 14). Another series, Nosepickers, is great for elementary and middle school students (no experience with the subject matter needed—ooh!).

Lifesaver Tips

- The author speaks to audiences from Grades 2–12 but prefers younger high school students.

- The author will give up to three presentations per day.

- The author will conduct a personal writing workshop to help young adventure authors (up to twenty-five) hone their craft.

- Leave plenty of time for question-and-answer sessions at the end of his presentations. Korman is entertaining and funny and recently did a great job of answering our student questions with humor and wit! (Lifesaver Tool #59 is a list of top 10 questions and answers.)

- Invite as many students as possible. Unlike many authors, Korman has no problem with large audiences. In fact, we recently hosted three hundred students, and Korman did a great job of interacting with our large, high-school audience.

Lifesaver Tweaks

- *Liar, Liar Pants on Fire* (Scholastic, 1999) is a great book to focus on for a primary author visit (Grades K–2).

- The Nosepickers series (Scholastic, 1999) is great for upper elementary and junior high students. "Pick" this one!

Lifesaver Trip #59

http://www.gordonkorman.com/

Dive into this author's site here. It's an adventure!

Gordon Answers the Top Ten Questions Kids Ask by Author Gordon Korman

http://www.gordonkorman.com/top10qna.htm

10. Did you really write your first book in seventh grade?

Yes, but it wasn't on purpose. In my school, the track and field coach had to teach language arts, and for writing, he just told us to work on whatever we wanted for the rest of the year. I wrote *This Can't Be Happening at Macdonald Hall*, which was published a year and a half later when I was fourteen.

9. Where do you get your ideas?

It's a combination between real life and pure imagination. I always start off with something real, but then I unleash my imagination to make it funnier, more interesting, and a better story. To be honest, by the time a book is done, you can't recognize much of the real-life part. It's been changed too much. But I never could have gotten there without it.

8. How much money do you make?

You knew it was coming—the number one question kids ask. So let's get it out of the way. I earn less than Shaquille O'Neal but more than the French-fry-box unfolder at the local Drive-Thru. I'm in that gray area.

7. What is your connection to the Disney TV series *The Jersey*?

I wrote The Monday Night Football Club novels, the book series *The Jersey* is based on. Beyond that, I don't really have any official role in the TV show, except as a viewer.

6. What is your nickname?

One of the reasons I wrote *The Sixth Grade Nickname Game* was that I hardly ever got cool nicknames as a kid—Gordie, Gord-o—nothing too creative. But when I was in sixth grade I was the G-Man. I loved it. I've been waiting twenty-five years to get another nickname that good.

5. What did you want to be before you became a writer?

When I was two years old, I wanted to be a dog when I grew up. I don't actually remember this, but my parents tell me that I used to eat dinner under the table in preparation for this career. Good thing I wound up a writer. I never could have gotten into the union.

Lifesaver Tool #59

4. Which book was the hardest to write?

The Island trilogy was a real challenge for me because I had to switch gears from comedy to action/adventure. Here were six shipwrecked kids who were in real danger of dying every minute. That's not the time to be cracking jokes. So it's not humor that keeps the reader turning pages; it's suspense and fear.

3. Do you have any pet peeves?

Opera, New York traffic, zucchini sticks, and books where the dog dies.

2. What is your most embarrassing moment?

When I was seventeen, I won the Air Canada Award for the most promising young writer in Canada. I wasn't used to wearing ties back then. (I still don't love them.) At the awards dinner, I stood up when my name was called. Then I sat back down again—dipping my tie right into the gravy! But don't worry, there were only four hundred and fifty people watching.

1. What is the answer to all the world's problems?

Come on, how could I know that? But I do believe in the power of a good sense of humor. Laughter may not solve anything, but it sure makes the bad stuff a lot easier to take. So maybe the answer to all the world's problems is: keep on laughing!

Lifesaver Tool #59

Literacy Lifesaver #60

"Been There, Done That!"

Congratulations! Your author visit is over (insert sigh of relief here!), and you can now sit back and celebrate your hard work and accomplishments. In this Literacy Lifesaver, you will find some tips on wrapping up the project, while keeping the students involved and interested in reading and writing. It is also important to conduct an evaluation while the visit is still fresh in the minds of students, staff, and parents. Don't miss the opportunity to learn what worked and, unfortunately, what didn't! (OK, it may be too early to start planning the next visit!)

Lifesaver Tips

- Be creative with writing your author thank-you letters! Interactive writing, shared writing, homemade greeting cards, and scrapbooking can all be fun alternatives to the typical thank-you letter.

- Remember, however, that some teachers will want to use this opportunity to teach letter writing because it is a standard and it helps to have a purpose for writing.

- Continue to promote author studies through special sections of the library where additional titles are available and ready for checkout.

- Utilize the library as a place to display projects from the author's books!

- Collaborate with teachers on creating additional units of study on book titles that interested the students during the visit but you haven't previously found time to investigate.

- Work with teachers on writing workshop mini-lessons using the author's works and sharing his or her language.

- Utilize Lifesaver Tool #60 to evaluate the visit. Encourage all stakeholders to participate in the evaluation process.

Lifesaver Trip #60

http://www.education-world.com/a_curr/curr374.shtml

This Web site includes a wealth of information on planning an author's visit. In addition, you will find information on *Terrific Connections with Authors, Illustrators, and Storytellers* (Libraries Unlimited, 1999), which includes everything you need to prepare, prepare, and prepare some more for your upcoming author visit!

Visiting Author Evaluation Form

Please circle your role:

Parent/Community Member   Teacher   Staff Member   Student/Classroom

Author:

Date of Visit:

On a scale from 1 to 5 (with 1 being unsatisfactory and 5 being the best), please rate the author visit on the following statements:

1. The author was entertaining and connected to the audience.   1   2   3   4   5

2. Students were motivated and are reading/writing more.   1   2   3   4   5

3. The visit was well organized.   1   2   3   4   5

4. Students learned important information from the visit.   1   2   3   4   5

5. The author modeled a love for reading or writing.   1   2   3   4   5

Comments/Suggestions:

Lifesaver Tool #60

Lifesaver Notes

_____

_____

_____

_____

_____

_____

_____

_____

_____

_____

_____

_____

_____

_____

_____

_____

_____

_____

_____

_____

_____

_____

_____

Lifesaver Notes

Chapter 7

Independent Learning and Workstations

Introduction: Stations! All Aboard!

The "station" approach has been used very successfully in elementary school classrooms for years. Only recently have stations been used as a regular part of instruction at the middle school level; stations are still not standard practice in high school classrooms and even less used in the media center. When you "sea" the high levels of student engagement as they work independently at stations to complete essential tasks, you'll want to dive right into implementing library literacy stations!

Each Literacy Lifesaver in this chapter includes one station idea for a library literacy skill. For beginners, the station approach will simply be using the same idea (Lifesaver Tool) with small groups (all doing the same thing at the same time in small groups). For the more experienced station director, you can use all of the Lifesavers at one time in small groups and rotate.

The Station Approach: Get on Track

Before you can begin using library literacy stations, you need to get your feet wet about stations in general. The following questions and answers can help you "sea" what stations are all about.

After selecting the information literacy standard that you want to meet and teaching this in a whole-group format, stations provide a great way to practice the skill with less support from the teacher or librarian.

Why Use Stations?

After students have learned material that has been explicitly taught to the whole group and then used in guided practice, stations provide a great opportunity for independent practice of the skills (this is what stations are all about).

What Are Stations?

Stations are simply a structured approach to provide small-group, independent practice time.

How Can They Be Used?

Stations can be used with any content area or grade level—even in the media center!

What Do You Need to Know to Get Started?

See the Lifesaver Tips below for station survival.

Lifesaver Tips

- Carefully review information literacy standards.

- Select standards that you need to meet skills that may be lacking.

- Observe classes that use the station approach to see the strategy in action.

- Collaborate with the classroom teacher on essential skills that are needed.

- Gather resources, prepare materials, and develop procedures and routines for each station.

- Schedule time to teach, model, and practice each station prior to students' being released independently to the stations (allow ample time—you'll need several library periods before station launching).

- Collaborate with the teacher to assign collaborative heterogeneous student groups.

- Develop a form for observational assessment at stations (see Lifesaver Tool #61).

- Dive in!

- Monitor and adjust stations as needed.

- Be patient and persistent. This is a new approach for many students (and for you!).

- Review and reflect on observational notes with your collaborative partner.

- Make modifications and improvements for when the next train leaves the station!

Lifesaver Tweaks

Although the preceding tips are appropriate at all levels (K–12), tweaks may be needed at the individual classroom or library level. For example, some groups may need to be smaller, some larger. In some cases, you may want to split the station groups with your collaborative partner. Again, these tweaks are individual to the group's needs, and most will be on-the-spot modifications made as a result of your observational assessment.

As you become more comfortable implementing stations, you can have multiple stations (rather than just different groups working on the same station) and students rotating between the standards or skill-based lessons.

Lifesaver Trip #61

http://www.ala.org/ala/aasl/aaslproftools/learningstandards/standards.cfm

Find the American Association of School Librarians' new Standards for the 21st-Century Learner here. You'll also find discussion boards and blogs so that you can get survival tips from other media specialists who are diving into the station approach!

All Aboard!
Media Center Stations Observational Checklist

Students were on task during the stations.   1   2   3   4   5

(List students who needed redirection.)

The stations were at the correct level of difficulty. 1   2   3   4   5

(List recommendations for modifications.)

Student groups were appropriate.   1   2   3   4   5

(List suggestions for changes to groups.)

Students enjoyed the station approach.   1   2   3   4   5

(List comments as appropriate.)

*Students were observed applying the skill during future library visits.   Yes   No

(*Note: Save this tool to observe students in future library visits. List specific positives or concerns for making station modifications on the back of this sheet.)

Lifesaver Tool #61

Work It Out: Using Work Boards in the Media Center

Classroom teachers who are effectively implementing the station approach use a work board to organize students for their groups and tasks. This same tool can be very beneficial to the library media specialist. A work board can be used to display which station each group will be working at on the day they visit the library (if there will be multiple stations). If each group will be doing the same station, the work board can still be used effectively to keep track of which homeroom class has completed each of the stations. This tool really assists the media specialist with planning and keeping everyone "on track!"

Lifesaver Tips

- Collaborate with classroom teachers to determine the time that they have available for the units of study.

- Determine your plan. Will each station be based on a different information literacy standard in which the students will rotate or will each station be the same?

- Create your work board (see Lifesaver Tool #62).

- Organize your space to allow for multiple groups.

- Determine the role of the teacher. How will he or she assist you during station implementation? Will the teacher be "stationed" at a station, or, like you, be rotating between stations to get students back "on track"?

- Launch your stations! Choo-Choo!

Lifesaver Trip #62

http://www.jmeacham.com/centers/centers.workboard.htm

This site shows three examples of a classroom teacher's work board using various types of pocket charts.

STUDENT GROUPS	STATION ACTIVITIES
#1	BOOK SEARCHING
#2	JOURNAL WRITING
#3	INDEPENDENT READING
#4	RESEARCH

ABOVE: EXAMPLE OF A MEDIA CENTER WORK BOARD.

NOTE: The stations (at right) will remain the same; however, the station tasks will change.

TIPS: If a pocket chart is used for the work board (above), the groups can easily be rotated (and group members changed as needed).

Lifesaver Tool #62

Literacy Lifesaver #63

"I Don't Believe It!"

One of the most important skills for primary students is understanding the difference between fiction and nonfiction. Utilizing the station approach to provide independent practice of this skill will be a great support not only in meeting library standards but in meeting classroom standards as well. Several lifesaver trips will allow you to collaborate with your classroom teachers on some of the best information and resources for the nonfiction genre.

Lifesaver Tips

- Select one of your favorite fictional read-alouds.

- Find a nonfiction book to partner with your selection that provides information on your theme.

- Explicitly teach students the vocabulary: fiction, nonfiction, real, make-believe, true, false, facts, and so on.

- Read aloud each book while stopping to think out loud at key points to state the key vocabulary (depending on the time available, this may take more than one library session).

- Create a chart for fiction and nonfiction to reinforce the concepts from your read aloud. (Examples: "Was this character real?" "Would that go on our nonfiction chart or fiction chart?")

- When students appear to understand the concept, teach the station expectations and model Literacy Tool #63.1 (fiction) and #63.2 (nonfiction).

- Implement the stations and monitor groups.

- Collaborate with the classroom teacher on literacy stations that she or he may use in the classroom to reinforce this skill.

Lifesaver Trip #63

http://teacher.scholastic.com/products/classroombooks/nonfiction.asp

This site addresses the concerns of the nonfiction gap in our classrooms and libraries. A variety of resources are available as part of a leveled library that media specialists can order to support classroom instruction or as part of the station approach for teaching this unit.

http://library.thinkquest.org/5002/Basic/ficnf.htm

Check out this PowerPoint presentation created by sixth graders as part of a unit to teach the important standard of fiction and nonfiction.

http://www.encyclopedia.com/doc/1G1-84344608.html

This site includes a wealth of information on the importance of pairing fiction and nonfiction texts to aid in reading comprehension.

http://www.le.ac.uk/engassoc/primary/NF1.html

This site is a must-see for researching information and accessing the best resources for nonfiction children's literature!

"I Don't Believe It!" Station Activity

Group Name_____

Fiction
List three things that "can't really happen."

"I Don't Believe It!" Station Activity

Group Name_____

Nonfiction
List three real facts.

Literacy Lifesaver #64

Book Looks!

One of the key skills for primary students is to learn the parts of a book. This is also an important part of kindergarten and first-grade assessment in the classroom as part of the "concepts of print" assessment. By collaborating with the classroom teacher, you can greatly support students in this skill area, especially those who haven't had the "lap time" of someone reading to them at home.

Lifesaver Tips

- Collaborate with the classroom teacher to determine students who will need additional support with this unit.

- Introduce the key vocabulary by writing it on index cards (or Post-It notes) and placing it on a "real book" to help students locate the information and become familiar with the words.

- Encourage the classroom teacher to model this skill with read-alouds in the classroom.

- Review Lifesaver Tool #64 to determine whether you would like each group to complete the activity sheet based on selected books at their station, or if you would prefer to cut apart the sheet and have each group focus on one part at a time with the groups rotating.

- Consider having younger students write on sentence strips.

- Utilize the activity sheet for modeling on the overhead projector prior to station work as guided practice.

- Organize students into heterogeneous groups to ensure success for all.

- Consider using the draw and/or write strategy as an extension in the classroom after students have completed the stations.

Lifesaver Trip #64

http://www.nationalserviceresources.org/learns/literacy-print

This trip is especially helpful for training volunteers and tutors to work with students on learning the different parts of a book.

http://www-tep.ucsd.edu/courses/eds361b/WI08/361Blect1.ppt#1

This trip contains invaluable information for teachers, librarians, or even parents who are new to kindergarten or first grade!

Look at a Book!

Can you find my parts?

B   Books are fun for you to read.

O   Open me, and I will plant a seed.

O   Out of me comes things that you need to know.

K   Keep learning so that you will grow and grow!

Book #_____

1.   What is my title?

_____

2.   What is the call number on my spine?

_____

3.   Who wrote me? (Author)

_____

4.   Who drew my pictures? (Illustrator)

_____

5.   Do I have a table of contents?   Yes   No

6.   Do I have an index or a glossary?   Yes   No

On the back of this paper, draw or write one thing that you learned from me.

Lifesaver Tool #64

Literacy Lifesaver #65

"Dewey" Know Our Favorite Authors?

At the primary level, a great way for students to be introduced to the Dewey Decimal System is by finding their favorite authors. This unit is most effective when collaboration exists between the media specialist and classroom teacher. When students are introduced to author studies as part of a great read-aloud program, both in the classroom and library, this unit provides students with the skills to access quickly the books that they need. As more teachers utilize "mentor texts" as part of their literacy instruction (especially in the writer's workshop), students will be looking for their favorite authors and will need independence with this task. Help your students to "dive in" with the following tips!

Lifesaver Tips

- Collaborate with the classroom teacher to determine which author studies have already been launched in the classroom.

- Assist teachers with ordering additional copies of read-alouds and consider organizing multiple copies into text sets for easy checkout by staff.

- Plan additional author studies for read-alouds during library time.

- Consider hosting an author visit or visit an author online (see the previous chapter of this book).

- Determine the time that you have available. Use Lifesaver Tool #65 with stations in the media center. If restricted for time, link with classrooms to encourage students to research their favorite authors and write "About the Author" responses during classroom station time. Explain that the winning work will be posted in the library in the appropriate (matching) Dewey section (see Lifesaver Tool #65).

- Collaborate with teachers to assess student writing and select the best work. Introduce the idea of call numbers and locating books by their Dewey Decimal number by modeling the posting of the "About the Author" winning pages in the correct section of the library. Add an index card with the correct Dewey Decimal number and headings.

- Consider grouping students into station groups for a scavenger hunt to look for the winning "About the Author" pages for student work posted around the media center from other classrooms.

- Observe students on future trips to the library to determine whether they are demonstrating more independence in locating their books.

Lifesaver Trip #65

http://www.harperchildrens.com/hch/picture/features/aliki/howabook/ book1.asp

This links features an adorable look at how a book is made from Aliki, a favorite author among the boys and girls.

About the Author Station Activity

Name or Group_____

Author_____

Book Title Selected _____

_____

Draw and Write what you like most about this author's book:

_____
_____
_____
_____
_____
_____

Dewey Decimal Number _____

Lifesaver Tool #65

Literacy Lifesaver #66

Out of "Cite!"

No matter the middle or high school, most students struggle with how to cite sources. Although technology has helped tremendously by providing online tools, students still struggle with how to cite sources correctly in a research paper or project. This Literacy Lifesaver will provide step-by-step directions for you to use the station approach to teaching students to cite Internet sources—out of cite!

Lifesaver Tips

Activity #1

Ask students to:

- Find three Internet sources on their chosen research topics.

- Print out (and staple, if needed) all sources.

- Highlight the following information on their Web page printouts: author's name (usually unavailable on Web page), page title (usually listed in bold at the top of the page; what the page is called), hosting site/organization (example: Wikipedia, AOL Music, whatever company is sponsoring the page), and the URL (http address).

Activity #2

Tell students to:

- Gather their highlighted sources.

- Go to http://www.citationmachine.net/.

- Click on MLA format (top left corner).

- Click on "Web document" (bottom left under "nonprint" sources).

- Fill in the blanks with the information they have highlighted from their printed Web page documents (some fields will be empty; this is fine).

- Change the date (if needed).

- Click on the "Submit" button (bottom of page).

- Review the completed citation in the gray box.

- Copy and paste the citation into a Word document and title it "Sources."

- Repeat the steps for all other sources.

Activity #3

Students should:

- Open "Sources" document.

- Change the title from "Sources" to "Works Cited."

- Double space document (there should be two spaces between citations).

- Make sure to "hang their authors" (second line is indented under the author's name, opposite of a regular paragraph indent).

- Put their sources in alphabetical order by the first word of each citation.

- Print and save their document.

- Use the "three before me" strategy. Students show their printouts to three classmates before they turn it in for grading. Students should review to make sure all steps are followed and provide helpful feedback to the author.

Note: As you can see by glancing at the homepage (refer to Lifesaver Trip #66), the Citation Machine can be used to automatically cite all other sources as well. I chose the Internet option because it seems to be the most popular source. For additional station options, you could have the students cite print materials (yes, there are books in the media center!).

Lifesaver Trip #66

http://www.citationmachine.org/

This is the home of Landmark's "Son of Citation Machine." This online citation tool is truly "out of cite!"

Out of "Cite!"
Citing Internet Web Sites

<u>Directions:</u> Fill in the blanks below to help you as you cite your sources using Landmark's "Son of Citation Machine" (http://www.citationmachine.net).

Author's Last Name_____

(often unavailable on Web sites)

Author's First Name_____

(often unavailable on Web sites)

Page Title_____

(title of the page, usually centered or in bold)

Site Title_____

(only use if different from page title above)

Organization/Host Site_____

(the company or group that "paid for" this site)

URL/http Address_____

(always starts with http://...)

Date You Looked Up Information_____

(not always today's date; refer to printout on bottom right for the correct date)

Note: The online citation tool will ask for other information that you may include later.

Lifesaver Tool #66

From *100+ Literacy Lifesavers: A Survival Guide for Librarians and Teachers K–12* by Pamela S. Bacon and Tammy K. Bacon. Westport, CT: Libraries Unlimited. Copyright © 2009.

Literacy Lifesaver #67

Library Tour and Explore

Once you get 'em in the door (sometimes the hardest part), they've got to be able to find what they're looking for. This Literacy Lifesaver is a hands-on project that is perfect for stations.

Lifesaver Tips

- Materials needed: construction paper, markers, scissors, glue, handouts (see Lifesaver Tool #67).

- Involve student library helpers in this project—it will be messy!

- Students can be divided into activity groups (see below) using the station approach, or you can work together in a whole group to complete the project (depending on your students and their level of independence).

- Hold a contest for the best project. Not only are the students learning where things are in the library, their completed projects are great visuals for other students to use.

- Frame winning projects (with credit) and post around the media center.

Activity #1

- As a whole-group or in small groups, brainstorm parts of the library students would expect to find.

- Narrow down the brainstorm list to the most important parts of the media center.

Activity #2

- Distribute handouts (Lifesaver Tool #67) and have students cut out and label parts of the media center.

Activity #3

- Send students throughout the media center to locate sections of the library.

Activity #4

- Cut and paste sections of the media center onto construction paper.
- Decorate completed maps.

Lifesaver Trip #67

http://_____

Insert your school library link here.

Students can explore your library virtually as another station option!

http://www.wayne.k12.in.us/bdmedia/index.htm

Sneak a peak at the media center at Pam's school. Go Giants!

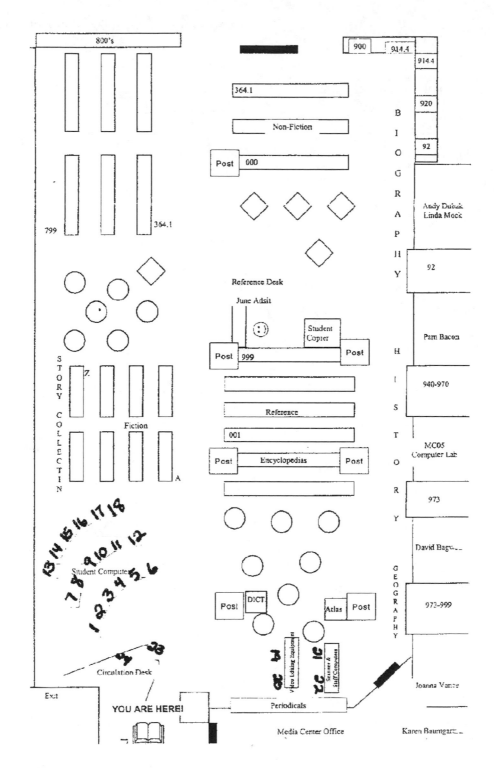

Note: Library map designed by Jennifer Kopsas

Lifesaver Tool #67

Book Pass

You've heard it before. Tim the Teacher swears his class only needs to check out books . . . and he doesn't need help. After all, students should be able to find books on their own, right? Hardly! Actually, effective book searching is a powerful literacy strategy that is often overlooked. Putting the right book into the right student's hands is one of the easiest—but also one of the hardest—ways that media specialists and teachers can collaborate to make important literacy gains. All too often, the teacher brings the class in to "get a book" with little pre-planning or thought. Before you know it, every student has checked out a book (usually the shortest ones, or ones within the closest reach from where those reluctant readers are sitting). Next time, before you let Tim and his class out to "sea" what great books you have, try this Read Around activity! Students are sure to catch a great book—and (who knows?) one they might even want to read.

Lifesaver Tips

- Gather a variety of high-interest books from different genres (five or six titles from each category—mystery, poetry, biography, sports, romance, fantasy—you decide!).

- Label station tables with different genres.

- Organize students into heterogeneous groups and send to stations.

- Set the timer for two minutes (younger students need more time!).

- Ask students to grab a book from their table. Do a picture walk of the front cover, read the back or the inside jacket flap, and get a feel for the book.

- When the timer goes off, the student puts the book down and completes the Read Around form (Lifesaver Tool #68).

- The teacher/librarian sets a timer for 1 minute (again, allow additional time for younger students).

- When the timer rings, students choose a different book from their table.

- Repeat the process.

- After five rounds, ask students to change stations.

- At the end of the class or time allowed, ask students to check out a book from among the choices.

Lifesaver Tweaks

- For primary students, ask an older student, parent volunteer, or media assistant to sit at each table to do a "picture walk" of the book with students and help complete the forms.

- Lifesaver Tool #68 could be enlarged and posted for ease of use with each group of younger students.

- Another option would be to use large chart paper to complete this activity as a shared or interactive writing activity in which the child shares the pen. The chart papers could then be taken back to the classroom and posted beside the book displays, making this collaborative activity link back to the classroom and promote rereading and recalling of important story topics among various genres.

- For primary students, the book genres might be more general, such as poetry, fiction, nonfiction, folktales, fairy tales.

- For more structure, ask students (young and old) to pick a number when they come in the classroom and go to that numbered table. When the bell rings, students would move in a clockwise rotation.

- For primary students, the teacher would bring the chosen books back to the classroom to use at literacy stations or other classroom activities.

- Need a tweak for middle grades? Go to http://www.lessonplanspage.com/ LAWhatIsGenre59.htm.

Lifesaver Trip #68

http://www.learnnc.org/lessons/annjenkins5232002118 (Primary)

This site provides a useful activity that could easily be used for review back in the classroom and provides an opportunity for assessment.

http://www.teenreads.com/ (Secondary)

This is one of the most amazing sites I've found that is both teen- and teacher-friendly. From reviews to raves, this site has it all!

Name _____

Read Around Rating Form

OPINION: Rate the book on a scale from 1 to 10

      1   2   3   4   5   6   7   8   9   10

Hated It ☹   So-So?   Loved It ☺

Title_____

Author_____

I/we liked this book because …

I/we did not like this book because …

Comments/other:

Lifesaver Tool #68

From *100+ Literacy Lifesavers: A Survival Guide for Librarians and Teachers K–12*
by Pamela S. Bacon and Tammy K. Bacon. Westport, CT: Libraries Unlimited. Copyright © 2009.

Literacy Lifesaver #69

We've Got Your Number!

It's hard to believe, but even after years of receiving library instruction on the Dewey Decimal System, many high school students still don't seem to have a clue what those numbers mean. This station approach to learning Dewey will get your students on board with the numbers (phone numbers for students in their group not included!).

Lifesaver Tips

- Divide students into ten groups (usually two or three students per group at the high school level).
- Have each student draw out a Dewey category (see Lifesaver Tool #69).
- Using large chart paper or an easel, mark the different sections of the media center with Dewey categories.
- Send students out to the Dewey location that they have drawn.
- Set a timer for three minutes. Students should search in their assigned section for the "best" book to represent their section and write the title on the chart paper or easel. Leave the book on a nearby table or counter for later use.
- After the timer goes off, students rotate clockwise to the next Dewey number. After thirty minutes (three minutes × ten Dewey stations), students will have visited each station and chosen books to best represent those Dewey categories.
- Bring students back together and have groups "debate" why their books are the best ones to represent their DDC category.
- Review call numbers on books pulled to reinforce the Dewey concept.

Lifesaver Trip #69

http://www.deweybrowse.org/

Use this trip either before or after stations to reinforce the Dewey Decimal Classification System. After showing, ask students, "Do We Know Dewey Now?" (Sorry, I couldn't help it!)

Dewey Drawing

Title_____

Author_____

Locate book and list Dewey Number from
the Spine _____

Dewey Drawing

Title_____

Author_____

Locate book and list Dewey Number from
the Spine _____

Lifesaver Tool #69

Literacy Lifesaver #70

Were We "On Track"?

After completing station activities, it's critical that the library media specialist collaborate with classroom teachers to determine the effectiveness of the stations and to reflect on changes for next year. As we all know, out of sight is out of mind. By having a more formal evaluation, you can easily file it and have it on hand to review when you're ready to climb back on board with these station activities next year.

Lifesaver Tips

- Don't be too hard on yourself! If this was your first time implementing stations, remember that change is messy and we all learn by taking risks.

- Utilize Lifesaver Tool #70 with teachers and for self-reflection as soon as possible so that you don't lose the opportunity for honest reflection while the information is fresh in your mind.

- Include the students in the evaluation whenever possible.

- Keep a materials and resources list handy so that you have an easy reference to supplies you need to add to your stations next year.

- Hold a collaboration session over the evaluation with classroom teachers to ensure open communication. Remember that sometimes written feedback can be interpreted differently than it was intended (just like e-mails)!

- Utilize the "Notes" pages at the end of the chapter to list additional authors, skills, and/or reminders to be added to stations for next year.

- Congratulate your hard work and take time to celebrate your work with stations!

Lifesaver Trip #70

http://www.thirteen.org/edonline/ntti/resources/workshops/managing_students/practice.html#collab

Although this chapter focused primarily on stations created by the media center specialist, this link includes ways to use computers effectively as stations. Helpful tips are included for suggestions to integrate technology through a station approach, regardless of how many computers you have available.

"Were We on Track?"
Station Evaluation for the Media Center

• The media specialist understands the concept of managed independent learning. He or she has arranged the classroom and materials to implement stations for the unit.

      1   2   3   4   5

• Students know the routines of following a work board independently and/or following the specific station directions. The directions were clear and easy to understand.

      1   2   3   4   5

• Students move to their stations quietly and efficiently. If rotating, transitions are smooth.

      1   2   3   4   5

• Routines for expectations were clearly modeled and taught.

      1   2   3   4   5

• There was a gradual release of responsibility. The whole group lesson was explicitly taught, and students had a chance for guided practice prior to working in station groups.

      1   2   3   4   5

Comments/Suggestions:

Lifesaver Tool #70

Lifesaver Notes

_____
_____
_____
_____
_____
_____
_____
_____
_____
_____
_____
_____
_____
_____
_____
_____
_____
_____
_____

Lifesaver Notes

_____

_____

_____

_____

_____

_____

_____

_____

_____

_____

_____

_____

_____

_____

_____

_____

_____

_____

_____

_____

_____

Chapter 8

Needs Assessment, Data, and Rubrics

Need to Know about Needs Assessments?

As teachers and librarians, we informally assess all the time, and monitor and adjust accordingly. The goal of our constant assessment is, and should be, to improve student achievement. There are times, though, when we need to conduct a more formal assessment for the purpose of data analysis. The big assessment buzz right now is that assessment should be *for* learning—not *of* learning. In other words, give your assessment, gather your data pieces, but then *use* that data to help guide your instruction.

Before you can get on board with needs assessments (and, by the way, No Child Left Behind mandates that we *all* get on board), you need to know the basics of the four W's (what, who, why, when) of assessments. The chart that follows gives you a quick check so that you'll have everything you need.

ASSESSMENT	WHAT?	WHO?	WHY?
Pre-assessment	Fast check of learning to determine whether immediate changes need to be made	All learners	To determine whether further individual assessments are needed
Prescriptive	Gather data to be used for analysis	Individual learners	To meet individual needs of students (esp. at-risk learners)
Progress report	Compare data to measure progress and report changes	Any learners not meeting standards	To assess whether students are making progress toward learning goals
Post-assessment	Summary data	All learners	To measure growth

Lifesaver Tips

- Use Lifesaver Tool #71 to gather reading assessment data. (We use the SRI at our school and track scores, but the template works for any type of reading assessment data.)

- If you're new to data gathering, talk to your principal. He or she is made aware of data workshops (especially those tied into school improvement) that can be just what you need to get started!

- Become familiar with Microsoft Excel's features. For example, the auto summary is a wonderful feature to calculate critical baseline data in an instant. The sorting features in Excel also make data work easier. (For example, you can easily switch back and forth between the alphabetical last name list and the numeric score list, depending on what data you're looking for.)

- Don't get overwhelmed. For the first year, just giving an assessment and storing the data might be enough. Then, when you're comfortable with that piece, you can actually begin to analyze the data.

- As the media specialist at our school, I have been heavily involved with data collection as a member of the school improvement team. There are many ways to play an important part in data collection, however. With high-stakes testing, any part you can do to improve student achievement will be even more critical in the future.

Lifesaver Trip #71

http://teacher.scholastic.com/products/sri/

Believe me, I'm not getting any kickbacks from Scholastic, but I simply must include the homepage for the SRI here. In terms of needs assessment and data collection, one of the best ways media specialists can get on board is by administering this reading assessment and collecting the results. Reading assessment is critical at any level (K–12) and the media specialist's role as a reading expert is just as critical. Jump on board and help your school where they need you most!

School Name_____

Teacher_____ Goal Area_____

Assessment Data Source (List Date)	Current Level (Pre-Test)	Final Level (Post-Test)	Met Goal

*Note: This template can be used for data assessment for program data or for individual student assessment data.

Lifesaver Tool #71

Literacy Lifesaver #72

Get It "Write!": A Primary Writing Assessment

Primary teachers have become great "kid watchers" in order to make instructional decisions based on informal observational assessment. Sometimes teachers and librarians feel (and rightly so) as if they are doing more assessment than actual instruction! Collaboration between librarians and teachers is the key to making the most of your effort and your limited time. Utilize the tips and tools that follow to make sure you get it "write" when supporting classroom teachers in analyzing and reflecting on student work samples. As a busy media specialist, it's obvious your time to collaborate on this type of writing assessment will be limited. However, any time you can assist with assessment, the better off your students will be—and the more indispensable you'll be as an instructional leader.

Lifesaver Tips

- Review grade-level writing standards and begin selecting appropriate read-aloud books to use as mentor texts (see your state's Department of Education Web site for specific grade-level standards).

- Collaborate with classroom teachers on which mini-lessons you can present during the class's library visit.

- Collaborate with classroom teachers to develop a monthly schedule and checklist for tracking and evaluating specific skills that will be assessed (see Lifesaver Trip #72 for a chart in Microsoft Word format). Be sure to include space for comments and observational notes.

- Consider co-teaching lessons in the classroom setting during writing workshop time (as time allows).

- Use Lifesaver Tool #72 for a blank co-planning assessment checklist.

- Assist teachers in assessing student writing by pair sharing of student work and selecting appropriate anchor papers to ensure consistency in expectations.

- Display student work whenever possible in the media center. This viewing opportunity makes students feel special!

- Utilize student examples (without names) to show examples for future mini-lessons. You can't save everything, but capturing the best of the best makes future lessons a breeze.

Lifesaver Trip #72

http://teachersnetwork.org/NTNY/nychelp/Literacy/asseswrite.htm

This site is an excellent resource for library media specialists to share with classroom teachers during professional development workshops that focus on utilizing assessment to drive instruction.

http://teachersnetwork.org/NTNY/nychelp/Literacy/Demas%20Chart.doc

This link takes you directly to the Lifesaver Chart mentioned earlier.

Co-Planning Assessment Checklist

Teacher(s)_____ Date_____

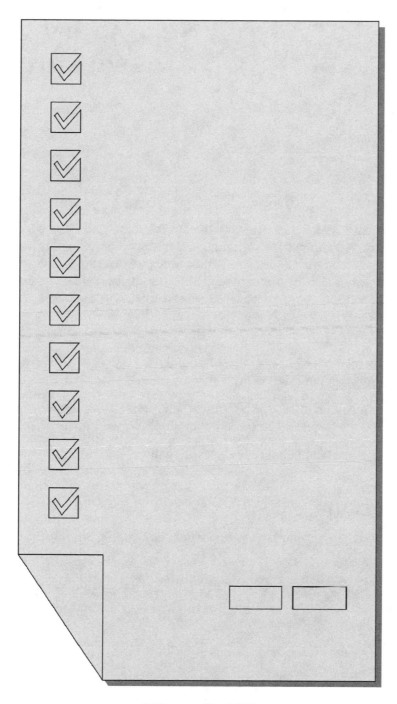

Lifesaver Tool #72

Literacy Lifesaver #73

"Write On!": A Secondary Writing Assessment

When secondary students used to visit the library, they would come to just "get a book" or, more recently, "use a computer." More and more often, we're seeing the trend move away from the basics and move toward quality instruction. Because students come to the media center to find quality books, it makes sense that the media specialist would also become involved in the assessment of locating the books when they find them.

Lifesaver Tips

- Use Lifesaver Tool #73 after you have conducted a library orientation, focusing on location of fiction and nonfiction books.

- This activity is an excellent individual and small-group assessment piece. For larger groups, the media specialist could divide the class with media assistants, if possible.

- Model the activity together before assigning the task to students to make sure everyone is "on board."

Lifesaver Trip # 73

http://www.teach-nology.com/worksheets/research/book/basic/

This quiz on the parts of a nonfiction book is just the assessment you'll need. You could use it for a pre-test (before you taught the lesson) and then a post-test (after you taught the lesson) to determine growth. Note: For upper-level students, you'll want to make it a little more challenging!

Name_____

Teacher_____ Date_____

Observational Assessment: Locating Information

• The student can scan for important information.	Yes	No
• The student can locate clues that help him/her understand the meaning of the story.	Yes	No
• The student rereads to find information.	Yes	No
• The student can locate headings and subheadings.	Yes	No
• The student can list the sequence of events.	Yes	No
• The student can make predictions of possible future events.	Yes	No

Other Observations:

Lifesaver Tool #73

From *100+ Literacy Lifesavers: A Survival Guide for Librarians and Teachers K–12*
by Pamela S. Bacon and Tammy K. Bacon. Westport, CT: Libraries Unlimited. Copyright © 2009.

We're in Control: Other Assessments

In today's fast-paced educational world, we media specialists must wear a variety of hats. While juggling literacy initiatives, technology integration, and professional development workshops, we almost need to put on armor to lead the change effort with school improvement teams and administrators. As change agents, we often wonder if we are on target—or if we, perhaps, are the target (sound familiar?). By employing the tips that follow, library media specialists can support classroom teachers by helping them to target specific goals and celebrate accomplishments throughout the year versus waiting on those annual—and often frustrating—state assessment results.

Lifesaver Tips

- Work with your school improvement team to determine which formative and summative assessments will be selected to monitor student achievement.

- Collaborate with teachers to develop a schedule for progress monitoring (see Lifesaver Tool #74).

- Assist teachers with data interpretation and reflection. New at this? Just ask a special education teacher (they're data analysis experts!).

- Set goals for co-teaching targeted intervention lessons with at-risk students.

- Ensure that teachers celebrate ongoing progress, even if students have not yet reached benchmark goals.

- Post results and lead collaboration sessions with grade-level teams to model the sharing of successful strategies.

Lifesaver Trip #74

http://www.nsdc.org/library/publications/jsd/stiggins202.cfm

This site is a must-see for librarians and teachers who are leading school improvement efforts in the area of assessment and instructional improvement.

```
100_____

90 _____

80 _____
```

Assessments: We're in Control!

Teacher/Grade Level _____

Assessment_____

Use this thermometer to chart the progress of your class or grade level for each benchmark assessment period.

Celebrate your accomplishments along the way! Remember that you are the thermostat and arc in control—not just a thermometer!

(Consider using a different color for each assessment period for easier viewing of the results).

```
70 _____

60 _____

50 _____

40 _____

30 _____

20 _____

10 _____
```

Lifesaver Tool #74

Literacy Lifesaver #75

Can We Talk?

Like it or not, library media specialists are often put in the public relations role, with or without the experience or skills needed for success. This section provides librarians with strategies for leading effective meetings, setting norms, and helping promote their school's student achievement progress.

Lifesaver Tips

- Meet with your administrator and school improvement team to plan a whole staff meeting on effective collaboration.

- Determine the role of each team member.

- Assess the needs of your staff with regards to effective communication.

- Brainstorm norms for effective communication, collaboration and problem solving.

- Develop strategies as a staff for how to resolve conflict and build trust.

- Set guidelines for effective meetings and collaboration sessions.

- Develop checklists or T-charts for what attendees would see and hear during an effective meeting (see Lifesaver Tool #75).

- Post the norms and expectations in areas where collaboration sessions will be held.

- Assist in sharing this information with key stakeholders and community members who assist on school improvement committees.

- Utilize Lifesaver Tool #75 as a reflection tool for observational assessment during future meetings to determine what progress has been made and as a way to determine where improvement is needed.

Lifesaver Trip #75

http://www.edu.gov.on.ca/eng/studentsuccess/thinkliteracy/files/SupportBookN ov2006final.pdf

This trip provides invaluable information to assist school improvement teams with strategies to discuss data and to help various stakeholders review data objectively during collaboration sessions. Although the example is specific to boys and literacy, the process of data interpretation and differentiating instruction is helpful for any data discussions. Dive in!

Can We Talk?

T-Chart for Effective Collaboration

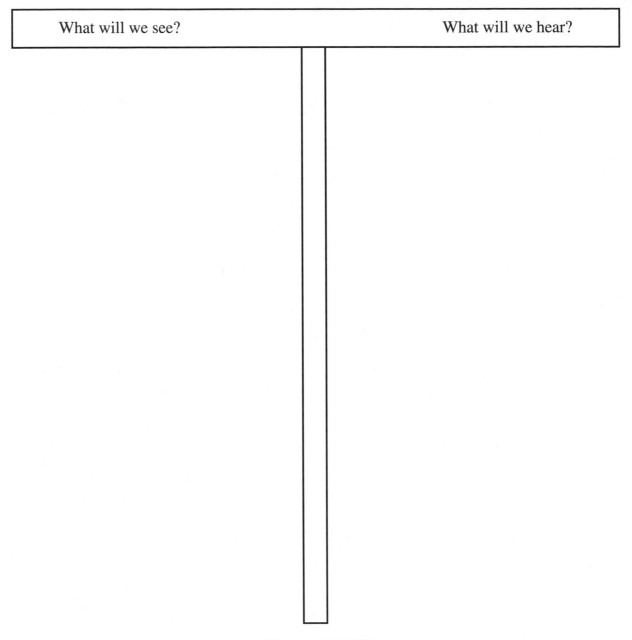

What will we see?	What will we hear?

Lifesaver Tool #75

Literacy Lifesaver #76

Reading Rubrics

There's no doubt about it—rubrics are truly assessment lifesavers! They're lifesavers for students because they know right up front how they will be graded (no surprises!). They're lifesavers for teachers and librarians because rubrics are such valuable timesavers. This lifesaver focuses on three of the best online rubric sites. Dive In!

Lifesaver Tips

- Rubistar: http://rubistar.4teachers.org/index.php

You'll be a "star" after you tell others about this awesome free site that enables teachers to create their own rubrics for project-based assessments. The site features ten searchable rubric links, including reading, writing, and multimedia. Although a quick registration is mandatory to access all the rubrics (you'll want to view others for ideas), the site is free and extremely user-friendly (we were able to complete a quality independent reading rubric in less than two minutes without registering!).

- Kathy Schrock's Guide for Educators: Teacher Helpers Assessment & Rubric Information (http://school.discoveryeducation.com/schrockguide/assess.html). Kathy has done it again—she's provided the perfect resources for all of our rubric needs! Find resources here to create your own rubric or customize a rubric that has already been created. Browse under subject-specific rubrics to find library and media-center-related rubrics. All the resources you need are here!

- Teachnology: http://www.teach-nology.com/web_tools/rubrics/

The self-proclaimed "You Asked for It, and We Made It!" site for rubrics. The Language Arts section of this online rubric site has nine clickable free rubrics for your use. There's a reading rubric, a writing rubric, and even a ready-to-use rubric for projects—all at the click of the mouse. This site features a teacher discussion board that has some quite lively debates (not all related to rubrics, by the way!).

- Lifesaver Tool #76 is an evaluation tool for rubrics you "sea" or create!

Lifesaver Trip #76

http://www.rubrics4teachers.com/

Quite a progressive little site, rubrics4teachers, even features a podcasting rubric (as well as one on dance!). You'll be able to dance out of the media center with all the time you've saved at this site. Anyone care to do The Swim?

http://www.relearning.org/resources/PDF/rubric_sampler.pdf

This site has it all for those who want to learn how to develop effective rubrics and use these tools to enhance your performance-based product. Its thirty-six pages may be a little overwhelming (many content-related examples are included) at first, so start with the first five pages for the basics on diving into rubrics.

R Ready to Use

U Understandable

B Based on a range of work samples

R Reliable descriptors

I Instant feedback

C Consistent criteria

Pair/Share Reflection:

Trade a rubric with a partner teacher and/or the media specialist to review it against the criteria above for a great way to get objective feedback for assessment rubrics.

Reflections/Suggestions:

_____

_____

_____

Lifesaver Tool #76

The Real Post-Its:
Data Walls

Data, data, data. Sure, the word "data" sounds impressive, but if you don't *do* anything with it, you're just throwing around numbers. The idea is that your data should do the work for you. A data wall is nothing more than posting your data on a wall so that your results can be seen and tracked by all interested parties. This lifesaver helps you (and your students) get motivated by making data real.

Lifesaver Tips

- Decide which data piece you want to assess, collect, and track (number of books read, classes with numbers of books overdue, students who pass a library orientation test, etc.).

- Use a format that can be updated quickly and easily as the data changes. (Lifesaver Tool #77 uses a color-coded pocket chart for making easy data changes and updates.)

- Choose a location for your data wall that is visible, but protected (can only be changed by you. Students may think it's funny to change numbers!).

- Take a picture of the data wall before removing it at the end of the year. Post pictures in a scrapbook for an easy, space-saving way to keep track of your successes.

Lifesaver Trip #77

http://ckingeducation.com/DWB/Making%20Data%20Walls%20Accessible.ppt

This is a good PowerPoint presentation on the basics of creating literacy data walls and data displays. Photographs of portable displays are presented with accompanying information.

http://www.ccsso.org/content/pdfs/FCS%200208%20sec.ppt#19

A photograph of a well-organized display board.

Data Wall Example

If you are searching for a way to bring the data down to the level of individual students, this example is a "teacher-friendly" way to track student progress.

Steps:

- Determine the data to be tracked.
- Purchase a tricolor pocket chart with red, yellow, and green sections with red representing below level, yellow representing on-level, and green representing above level.
- Write individual student names who are being monitored for intervention on index cards.
- Write the data and test results on the card. (You might want to consider using different colored pens for each of the assessment periods.)
- List specific interventions on the back of the card.
- At each assessment period, update the cards and determine whether students have moved up, down, or stayed at the same level.

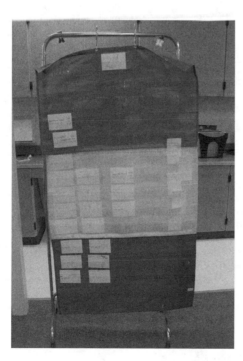

**Green- Top
(Above Level)**

**Yellow- Middle
(On Level)**

Red- Bottom

Lifesaver Tool #77

What's Up? Using Survey Data

Surveys are one way to find out what's up in the media center—and, unfortunately, what's not! As a library media specialist, you know that, right or wrong, program assessment is often linked to the perceptions of students, staff, parents, and community members. This section includes tips for creating surveys that not only assess perceptions but also assist librarians with program improvement based on survey data.

Lifesaver Tips

- Consider the following questions: Who will receive the survey? Who is your target audience? When will the survey be administered? How will the survey be distributed? How will the survey be collected? Who will analyze the data?

- Lifesaver Tool #78 is an example of a thirty-question media center survey that you can use to create your own customized survey.

- Consider color coding the surveys to represent different populations, one for students and another for staff (even if you give two different surveys, the color coding helps organize data collection).

- Analyze the data to determine strengths and weaknesses.

- Discuss data results with your "Friends of the Library" group.

- Collaborate with teachers and administrators to determine an action plan for program improvement.

Lifesaver Trip #78

http://nces.ed.gov/pubs2005/2005302.pdf

How does your school library media center measure up? Find out by comparing your library to others in the nation from the results of the 2002 U.S. Department of Education survey of School Library Media Centers.

http://dpi.wi.gov/tepdl/doc/pdslf10.doc

This resource site includes survey samples for all areas of school improvement. Beware! It is "deep" and you may want to focus on only one area, such as professional development, to keep from drowning in data!

http://goal.learningpt.org/datause/surveys/csssamp.asp?intCategoryID=1006

This site includes survey examples for program improvement.

Media Center Staff Survey

Name (optional) _____

1. What is your position?

2. If you have not used the Media Center this year, why not?

3. I brought my classes to the Media Center this year.

    Yes   No   Not Applicable

4. I co-planned or co-taught lessons with the media specialist this year.

    Yes   No   Not Applicable

5. Helping students become effective users of ideas and information is important.

    Disagree   Agree   Not sure

6. Students should be taught how to use information from a variety of formats.

    Disagree   Agree   Not sure

7. The Media Center plays an important part in the school's total educational program.

    Disagree   Agree   Not sure

8. The Media Center is vital to supporting students, instruction, and curriculum.

    Disagree   Agree   Not sure

9. I have input into the Media Center activities, policies, and materials purchased.

    Disagree   Agree   Not sure

10. The media specialist is approachable and open to collaboration ideas.

    Disagree   Agree   Not sure

Lifesaver Tool #78

11. The media specialist provides help to me on an individual basis.

     Disagree   Agree   Not sure

12. The media specialist is available for co-planning.

     Disagree   Agree   Not sure

13. The media specialist is available for co-teaching.

     Disagree   Agree   Not sure

14. The media specialist is available for co-evaluating.

     Disagree   Agree   Not sure

15. The media specialist plays a role in staff development.

     Disagree   Agree   Not sure

16. The media specialist is integral to our school's literacy and reading goals.

     Disagree   Agree   Not sure

17. The Media Center is adequately staffed.

     Disagree   Agree   Not sure

18. The Media Center staff is welcoming and helpful.

     Disagree   Agree   Not sure

19. The media specialist is welcoming and helpful.

     Disagree   Agree   Not sure

20. The Media Center provides a welcoming and inviting atmosphere.

     Disagree   Agree   Not sure

21. The learning climate in the Media Center is orderly and purposeful.

     Disagree   Agree   Not sure

Lifesaver Tool #78

22. I know how to schedule the use of the Media Center.

        Disagree   Agree   Not sure

23. The Media Center is adequately available for my own use.

        Disagree   Agree   Not sure

24. The Media Center is adequately available for use by individual students or small groups.

        Disagree   Agree   Not sure

25. The Media Center is adequately available for use by whole classes.

        Disagree   Agree   Not sure

26. The Media Center is open for a reasonable time during the school day.

        Disagree   Agree   Not sure

27. The Media Center is adequately available for extended hours beyond the school day.

        Disagree   Agree   Not sure

28. The resources in the Media Center are easy to locate and readily accessible.

        Disagree   Agree   Not sure

29. There are sufficient resources to support my curriculum and academic standards.

        Disagree   Agree   Not sure

30. Technology is effectively used in the Media Center.

        Disagree   Agree   Not sure

In the space below or on the back of this sheet, please list additional services, resources or programs that you would like for the Media Center to offer.

Lifesaver Tool #78

From *100+ Literacy Lifesavers: A Survival Guide for Librarians and Teachers K–12* by Pamela S. Bacon and Tammy K. Bacon. Westport, CT: Libraries Unlimited. Copyright © 2009.

Data, Data, and More Data!

Media specialists and teachers often feel like they are "drowning in the data." Which data should I collect? What is the most effective way to analyze it to make informed decisions? Will this work actually have a positive impact on student achievement? This section will provide tips and tools to assist media center specialists in helping to focus data collection on what matters most to simplify the process.

Lifesaver Tips

- Don't get overwhelmed. Start small and determine one or two key areas where you will begin collecting and analyzing data.

- Be consistent! Update your data on a regular, scheduled timeline.

- Collaborate with classroom teachers to analyze data and create displays to post the shared data, promoting your combined efforts.

- Use Lifesaver Trip #79 to brainstorm possibilities for data collection and to narrow your scope.

- Consider setting up an Excel spreadsheet using the second Lifesaver Trip that follows as a way to organize your data.

- Don't get stuck in a rut! Consider tracking different types of data that are still program-specific but give you another area of focus.

- Model the importance of celebrating all those small steps while you jump ahead in your data collection efforts.

Lifesaver Trip #79

http://homepage.mac.com/maryalicea/Sites/Anderson/MMS/data_gathering_9_04.pdf

Are you wondering what numbers to collect, and what to do with those numbers once you've got 'em? Dive into this Web site for practical advice on digging into the data and making it relevant.

http://www.mmischools.com/Articles/ReadArticle.aspx?ArticleID=10594

Are you wondering how to get started on creating a system to track your data? Check out this Web site with how-to steps for creating an Excel document to meet the needs of the media specialist.

http://www.schoollibrarymedia.com/articles/Logan2006v23n1.html

Are you looking for ways to involve students in data interpretation? Take a look at how one media specialist turned assessment and data collection into a meaningful way to make program decisions with student involvement.

School_____

Date_____

Working together with other staff members, use the chart below to brainstorm all of the current data that is being collected. Highlight areas in which the media specialist can best provide support.

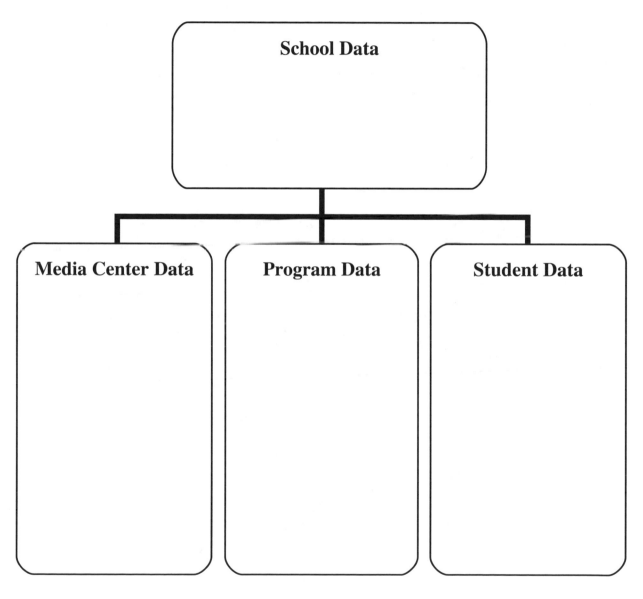

Lifesaver Tool #79

Literacy Lifesaver #80

High-Five Data and Assessment Resources

Finding the time to collect and analyze data is hard enough. You don't have the time to research and review the best data collection and assessment books as well. No worries—Pam has included her favorite top five resources here. Put the list to the assessment test!

Lifesaver Tips

- If you shop at Amazon.com, you can often get another similar book for a steal.

- If you offer to review the books for periodicals such as *School Library Journal* or *Library Media Connection*, you might be able to get the books for free!

- Because you only need these books for reference resources, ask your central office (or a partner library) to co-purchase some of the books with you for a substantial discount.

- Utilize the study group format for reading and reflecting over the resources.

- Be sure to select a recorder to document information from study groups that you want to include in future action plans.

- Use the jigsaw technique to share information with staff members.

- Consider meeting with other district librarians to share ideas and to divide tasks.

Lifesaver Trip #80

http://mlab.taik.fi/polut/Yhteisollinen/tyokalu_jigsaw.html

Puzzled about how to do a jigsaw? Find out here!

278

High Five: Pam's Pick of Data & Assessment Resources

Title: *Using Data to Improve Student Learning in High Schools*
Author: Victoria L. Bernhardt
Publisher: Eye on Education
Copyright: 2005
Cost: $49.95

Title: *Beyond the Numbers: Making Data Work for Teachers and School Leaders*
Author: Dr. Stephen White
Publisher: Lead and Learn Press
Copyright: 2005
Cost: $24.95

Title: *The Data Guidebook for Teachers and Leaders: Tools for Continuous Improvement*
Author: Eileen Depka
Publisher: Corwin Press
Copyright: 2006
Cost: $56.95

Title: *Action Plan for Outcomes Assessment in Your Library*
Author: Peter Hernon and Robert E. Dugan
Publisher: ALA
Copyright: 2002
Price: $55.00

Title: *Getting Excited about Data*
Author: Edie L. Holcomb
Publisher: Corwin Press
Copyright: 2004
Price: $38.95

Lifesaver Tool #80

Lifesaver Notes

_____

_____

_____

_____

_____

_____

_____

_____

_____

_____

_____

_____

_____

_____

_____

_____

_____

_____

_____

_____

_____

_____

Chapter 9

Graphic Organizers

Literacy Lifesaver #81

Let's Get Graphic

This chapter on graphic organizers is one that tends to be quite self-explanatory. However, we agreed that the main goal of our book would be to provide librarians and teachers with a variety of survival tools—and this chapter certainly meets that goal.

The beauty of graphic organizers is simple: they can be used and adapted to organize any content material or to fit any book. We hope these organizers will provide a springboard for your library and classroom collaboration.

This section includes both primary and secondary graphic organizers. For your survival, each graphic organizer focuses on a specific literacy strategy.

> Part I: Graphic Organizer Template (blank template to customize)

> Part II: Graphic Organizer with Book Focus (example of how graphic organizers can be used with a specific primary, intermediate, or secondary book)

Lifesaver Tips

- Literacy Skill Focus: Characterization

- Use this graphic organizer (Lifesaver Tool #81.1) with any novel that includes a strong character and a survival theme.

- Use this graphic organizer (see Lifesaver Tool #81.2) with *Tears of a Tiger* by Sharon Draper for a great example at the middle school level (or at the high school for reluctant readers).

Lifesaver Tweaks

- The lifesaver ring graphic organizer (Literacy Tool #81.1) can be enlarged for younger students who tend to write larger.

- Cut off the bottom half of Lifesaver Tool #81.1 before using with primary students (just the ring itself, Tam assures, will be more than enough!).

- Younger students can work together with the graphic organizer in small groups before working independently with their own tool.

Lifesaver Trip #81

http://www.learner.org/north/tm/ObservationHandouts.html.

This site includes an array of online graphic organizers (for K–12) that you won't have to "crane" your neck to find. The crane videos, pictures, and footage provides critical links to non-fiction examples for modeling thinking strategies with graphic organizers.

PROBLEM SOLVING IS A LIFESAVER!
DRAW A CONFLICT IN THE MIDDLE OF LIFESAVER RING!

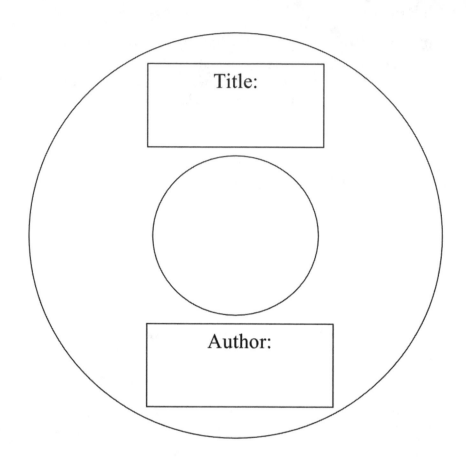

PROBLEM	SOLUTION

Lifesaver Tool #81.1

PROBLEM SOLVING IS A LIFESAVER!

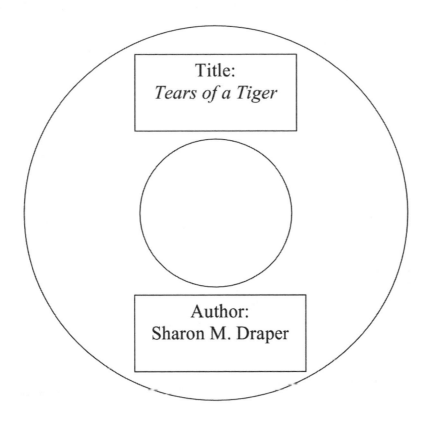

Title:
Tears of a Tiger

Author:
Sharon M. Draper

Draw a Conflict in the Middle of the Lifesaver Ring!

PROBLEM	SOLUTION
Andy, Rob, and his friends go out drinking after a basketball game.	Book Solution: Andy drives drunk, and Rob is killed. Better Solution: BJ is the designated driver.
Andy is depressed after his best friend is killed.	Book Solution: Andy commits suicide. Better Solution: Andy's parents take him to the hospital just in time.
Andy and his girlfriend fight.	Book Solution: They break up. Better Solution: They talk and work things out.

Lifesaver Tool #81.2

Literacy Lifesaver 82

A Chapter to Make You "Smile"

A great way for the library media specialist to support primary teachers is by launching interactive read-alouds in the media center and modeling the use of graphic organizers as a way to organize their thinking. The activity can then be easily practiced in classroom literacy stations using the same book or a different one . The collaboration between the library and the classroom thus creates a seamless transition of literacy skills.

Lifesaver Tips

- Literacy Skill Focus: Personification

- Use a great read-aloud such as *October Smiled Back* by Lisa Westberg Peters.

- Introduce the skill of personification, and have students listen for examples.

- Have students turn and talk during several parts of the story to share examples of personification by the author.

- Lifesaver Tool #82.1 can help you model an example directly from the story.

- Allow students some individual think time to come up with their own idea of how their favorite month could be used to show personification.

- Pick a student to share his or her idea and demonstrate on the overhead or presentation screen (see Lifesaver Tool #82.2).

- Continue sharing examples as time allows.

Lifesaver Tweaks

- Divide this lesson into two sessions with the launch in the media center and the follow-through in the classroom.

- Provide book and sample graphic organizers for students to use for independent practice in stations.

- Consider providing time for guided practice in the library or classroom by having small groups create examples.

- Provide ample sharing time in the classroom or library to provide presentation time with their work.

Lifesaver Trip #82

**http://www.edhelper.com/teachers/graphic_organizers.htm?gclid=
CMzRouCExY0CFQMYFQodgkUJLQ**

Check out the great reproducible graphic organizers available on this site. There are a variety available to meet the needs of library skill or classroom literacy standards.

Name_____ Date_____

Sketch a picture in the box below.

_____

_____

_____

_____

_____

_____

_____

Lifesaver Tool #82.1

Name_____ Date_____

Sketch a picture in the box below.

December is like a black penguin wobbling in search of food in the winter.

Wobble   Wobble   Wobble!

Lifesaver Tool #82.2

Literacy Lifesaver #83

Fall into Great Graphic Organizers

As you know, primary students benefit from having multiple opportunities to respond to texts in interesting and engaging ways. By collaborating with the classroom teacher, you can integrate this important skill into read-aloud extensions.

Lifesaver Tips

- Literacy Skill Focus: Author's Purpose

- Use a powerful mentor text, such as *Red Leaf, Yellow Leaf* by Lois Ehlert to integrate nonfiction while modeling writing examples.

- Begin by sharing this beautiful book with students as an interactive read-aloud.

- Point out the nonfiction section at the back of the book.

- Introduce the skill of determining the author's purpose (supported by Lifesaver Tool #83.2)

- Have students turn to each other and talk at the end of the story. Why does the author end the story with the question, "Can you guess why?"

- Have students predict why the author wants us to visit her tree in the fall.

Lifesaver Tweaks

- Use interactive writing with students as a way to model a written response.

- Use Lifesaver Tool #83.1 for guided practice utilizing shared writing.

- Lifesaver Tool #83.2 is an example to use either as a teacher resource or for a quick demonstration with students.

- Revisit the book to review sequencing and the nonfiction elements of the story.

- Encourage students to practice the skill during writing workshop time in the classroom or during literacy station time.

Lifesaver Trip #83

http://www.eduplace.com/graphicorganizer/

Scholastic provides educators with some of the best graphic organizers we have ever seen! If you can't find it here, it doesn't exist (or perhaps you can use our lifesaver tools!).

Name_____

Title

Author

Line 1

Line 2

Line 3

Line 4

Lifesaver Tool #83.1

Name_____

Can you guess why?
(Adapted from *Red Leaf, Yellow Leaf*)

Author (Insert Student Name or Class Name)

Trees are absolutely beautiful in the fall.

You can plant trees from seeds or from a twirly-whirly.

The leaves then change into bold and beautiful COLORS!

Colorful, Colorful Leaves!
(*change text to color for screen*)

Lifesaver Tool #83.2

Literacy Lifesaver #84

"Make a Good Choice"

Primary teachers will greatly appreciate the opportunity to collaborate with the library media specialist to help their students learn ways to solve conflicts and make good choices. With time being a precious resource in both the media center and the classroom, collaborative units help make every minute count.

Lifesaver Tips

- Literacy Skill Focus: Conflict Resolution, Problem-Solving

- Begin unit with a great read-aloud, such as *Stand Tall Molly Lou Melon* by Patty Lovell.

- Pause frequently during the read-aloud to allow students to turn and talk about the choices that Molly makes. What would they do if they were Molly?

- Use Lifesaver Tool #84.1 to brainstorm ideas following the first reading of the story.

- Share Lifesaver Tool #84.2 with the classroom teacher to provide follow-up opportunities with students in the classroom.

- Use this graphic organizer with other character-related stories to reinforce citizenship skills.

Lifesaver Tweaks

- Create citizenship charts for different storybook characters. What can we learn from these characters?

- Plan cooperative learning activities with each group using a different read-aloud that has been previously taught. Use Lifesaver Tool #84.1 to record ideas.

- Utilize read-aloud stories in the classroom for literacy station activities.

- Consider selecting students to share ideas on the school announcements to reinforce good choices.

- Post exemplary examples of completed graphic organizers in the media center to showcase student work.

Lifesaver Trip #84

http://www.sdcoe.k12.ca.us/score/actbank/torganiz.htm

This site provides several reproducible graphic organizers. We have found the "cycle" organizer to be a terrific tool to be used for many different purposes.

Name_____

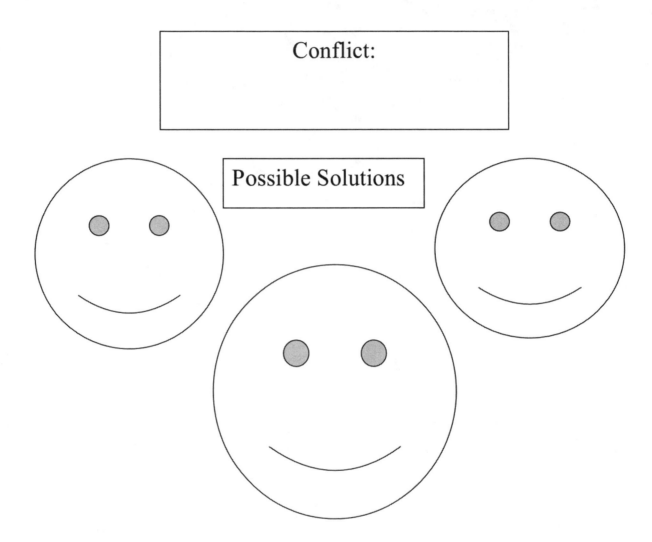

Conflict:

Possible Solutions

Name_____

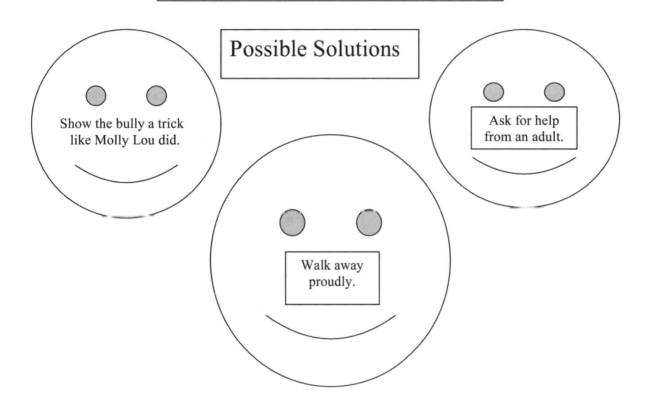

Conflict: ☹
The bully teases Molly Lou about her buck teeth.

Possible Solutions

Show the bully a trick like Molly Lou did.

Ask for help from an adult.

Walk away proudly.

Lifesaver Tool #84.2

Literacy Lifesaver #85

It's "Important!"

One of the most important literacy skills that primary students need to learn is the comprehension skill of understanding the main idea of the story. In addition, students need the opportunity to practice retelling stories with what the story is "mostly about" and what supporting details were included. As a library media specialist, you can easily launch this lesson with a great mentor text and then collaborate with the classroom teacher on ways to reinforce this comprehension skill in the classroom.

Lifesaver Tips

- Literacy Skill Focus: Main Idea

- Read aloud *The Important Book* by Margaret Wise Brown.

- Use Lifesaver Tool #85.1 and #85.2 to demonstrate the main idea and the supporting details in the story.

- Have students practice orally retelling the story to partners.

- Divide students into cooperative groups to practice with the graphic organizer (Lifesaver Tool #85.1) on specific pages from the story.

- Have students share the graphic organizers they created in small groups with the large group.

Lifesaver Tweaks

- Provide frequent opportunities to model this important skill by doing a "think aloud" with other read-aloud stories.

- Practice the skill with a shared writing activity on chart paper.

- Continue to practice this skill area with response journals.

- Review the skill of retelling often, especially before students are given individual reading assessments in the classroom.

Lifesaver Trip #85

http://www.k111.k12.il.us/lafayette/fourblocks/graphic_organizers.htm

This Four-Block site provides several graphic organizers to be used in their balanced literacy framework.

Main Idea:

Supporting Detail #1:

Supporting Detail #2:

Supporting Detail #3:

Restate Main Idea:

Lifesaver Tool #85.1

Main Idea:
The important thing about the wind is that it blows.

Supporting Detail #1:
You can't see it.

Supporting Detail #2:
You can feel it on your cheek.

Supporting Detail #3:
It blows hats away and it blows sailboats.

Restate Main Idea:
The important thing about the wind is that it blows.

Lifesaver Tool #85.2

Literacy Lifesaver #86

Opposites Attract!

A great way for the library media specialist to collaborate with classroom teachers is through shared word study units. Students will become proficient at noticing strong words through the modeling of the two educators working together to build students' background and vocabulary knowledge. Great mentor texts level the playing field for all children to move forward in their literacy learning.

Lifesaver Tips

- Literacy Skill Focus: Vocabulary and Suffixes

- Introduce students to a great read-aloud such as *Hottest Coldest Highest Deepest* by Steve Jenkins.

- Share the key nonfiction elements of the book including graphs, maps, and diagrams to provide students with a deeper understanding of the book.

- Review the word-building skill of opposites with the students.

- Chart words from the story on Lifesaver Tool #86.1 as you model examples.

Lifesaver Tweaks

- Use Lifesaver Tool #86.2 with students to review the book, or have the classroom teacher use it as she reteaches the skill during word work time.

- Use Lifesaver Tool #86.1 with another read-aloud in the classroom to provide additional guided practice time with students.

- Provide a variety of texts for students to use with the graphic organizer during literacy work stations.

- Create "Opposites Attract" charts to post around the classroom or media center.

Lifesaver Trip #86

This site provides a great resource for word study units and includes examples of graphic organizers to integrate vocabulary study.

http://www.perfectionlearning.com/images/products/pdfs/vlit/vwp.tg.4.pdf

Name_____

Opposites Attract!

List word partners on the arrows below.

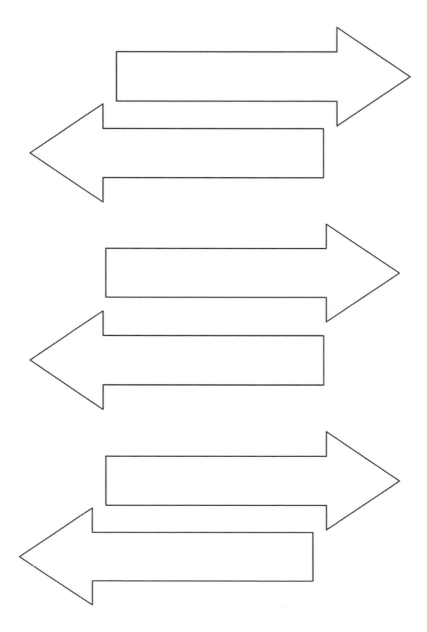

Lifesaver Tool #86.1

Name_____

<table>
<tr><td>

Opposites Attract!

List word partners on the arrows below.

</td></tr>
</table>

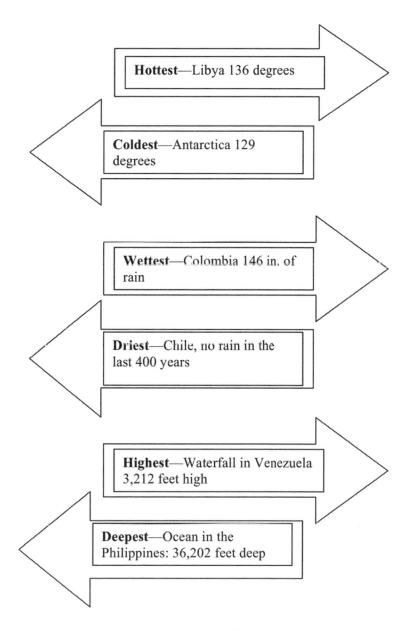

Hottest—Libya 136 degrees

Coldest—Antarctica 129 degrees

Wettest—Colombia 146 in. of rain

Driest—Chile, no rain in the last 400 years

Highest—Waterfall in Venezuela 3,212 feet high

Deepest—Ocean in the Philippines: 36,202 feet deep

Lifesaver Tool #86.1

Literacy Lifesaver #87

PCTSC—What Does It Mean?

There's nothing like a great mnemonic device to help students remember things (too bad I've never thought of one for bringing back library books!). This graphic organizer is a great tool to help students remember key story elements (plot, character, theme, setting, and conflict). Best of all, because PCTSC stands for "Please Come To Science Class," the science teachers now love me! Unfortunately, I couldn't make it work for library!

Lifesaver Tips

- Literacy Skill Focus: Story Elements

- Use mnemonics whenever you can to help your students remember important information.

- Use graphic organizers whenever you can to help students think visually and more deeply about a topic.

Lifesaver Tweaks

- Use only one or two of the letters (PCTSC) with younger students.

- Model the use of the graphic organizer (Lifesaver Tool #87.1) with younger intermediate students.

- Use the graphic organizer (see Lifesaver Tool #87.2) with high school students. This is customized to go with *Shooter* by Walter Dean Myers (fiction with nonfiction elements).

- Use the Presenstation or overhead and complete the graphic organizer with primary students.

Lifesaver Trip #87

http://www.greece.k12.ny.us/instruction/ela/6-12/Tools/Index.htm

A variety of graphic organizer templates, compiled by Greece Central School District (Rochester, New York), are provided on this site to encourage students to interact with text and engage in higher-level thinking skills. It's truly the most amazing resource we've come across in a long time!

Name _____

Class _____

P   Plot

C   Characters

T   Theme

S   Setting

C   Conflict(s)

Lifesaver Tool #87.1

Name _____

Class _____

Shooter Graphic Organizer

P Plot

Example: A school shooting takes place in a high school, and Cameron is being questioned.

C Characters

T Theme

S Setting

C Conflict(s)

Lifesaver Tool #87.2

Chain of Events

Who doesn't love a great paper-chain activity? This Literacy Lifesaver can be used with any grade level and adapted for any book or content area. Even high school students like seeing how long they can get their chain of events!

Lifesaver Tips

- Literacy Skill Focus: Plot, Cause, and Effect

- Use colored construction paper.

- Use a separate chain for each plot event (see Lifesaver Tool #88.1 for blank template).

- Hang individual paper chains from the ceiling, or group them together and hang around the room!

Lifesaver Tweaks

- Use one chain for a cause, use another for an effect (see Lifesaver Tool #88.2 for a book-related example using *Speak* by Laurie Halse Anderson).

- Use a different color of link between each student chain before hanging.

- Use this literacy activity as a challenge activity. Hang chains in the media center and see which class can have the most by the year's end!

Lifesaver Trip #88

http://www.richmond.k12.va.us/readamillion/graphicorganizers.htm

This site is truly amazing. Although some of the links are inactive, the ones that are still active make this site worth diving into. You can even find out how to create graphic organizers using PowerPoint (Note: paper chains not included!).

Cause and Effect Paper Chain Activity

Cause

Effect

Cause

Effect

Lifesaver Tool #88.1

Speak Paper Chain Activity

Cause

Melinda was so afraid to talk about what happened.

Effect

Melinda became unable to speak at all.

Cause

Effect

Lifesaver Tool #88.2

Literacy Lifesaver #89

It's a Date: Using Literacy Calendars

One of the most useful skills we can teach our students is organization. Organization of information is perhaps the biggest strength of graphic organizers. This graphic organizer is in calendar format and has as many uses as there are days in the year!

Lifesaver Tips

- Literacy Skill Focus: Vocabulary

- Use the template (see Lifesaver Tool #89.1) for a place to keep new vocabulary words.

- Provide students with a different calendar each month (use different colors to help students visually organize their paperwork).

- Have students work together and choose the best calendar (i.e., the greatest variety of word choices) per group to post in the classroom.

Lifesaver Tweaks

- Use the graphic organizer to record a "Quote a Day."

- Record upcoming homework assignments, quizzes, and tests (perhaps this calendar could be copied on red paper to catch students' attention!).

- Use the graphic organizer to record summary thoughts at the end of each day for a quick closure/summarization activity.

Lifesaver Trip #89

http://www.writedesignonline.com/organizers

Use this site to integrate writing skills with a variety of excellent graphic organizer templates. Write on!

Name _____ CLASS_____

IT'S A DATE!

MONTH _____

Monday	Tuesday	Wednesday	Thursday	Friday

Lifesaver Tool #89.1

Name _____ CLASS_____

IT'S A DATE!
MONTH _____

Monday	Tuesday	Wednesday	Thursday	Friday
Simile	Metaphor	Plot	Setting	Character
Conflic	Theme	Irony	Dialogue	Rising action
Falling action	Resolution	Alliteration	Epilogue	Prologue

Lifesaver Tool #89.1

Literacy Lifesaver #90

What They Say...
What It Means

One of the hardest skills to teach (based on experience and state test scores) is making inferences. It's hard enough just to get the students to read and understand what is being said when the meaning is clear. It's even harder to get students to understand implied meaning and make inferences when they read. This graphic organizer helps by organizing thoughts graphically and making students think about what is said and, most importantly, what it means.

Lifesaver Tips

- Literacy Skill Focus: Inferencing

- Read aloud a section of the book together and model the use of the "What They Say/What They Mean" graphic organizer (see Lifesaver Tool #90.1).

- Use the think-aloud strategy (i.e., the teacher/librarian explicitly models the process out loud for students) whenever possible, with or without the graphic organizer, to build these critical thinking skills.

Lifesaver Tweaks

- The example provided is for secondary students, based on Sharon Draper's *Forged by Fire* (see Lifesaver Tool #90.2).

- For younger students, assign only one or two (of the four) examples independently, until they become more adept at this skill.

- Instead of writing what the character says, students could use the text boxes to practice writing their own dialogues.

Lifesaver Trip #90

http://learn.shorelineschools.org/kellogg/smcallister/documents/making_inferences.ppt

Students will learn to make inferences and have a good laugh at the same time with this great site. A PowerPoint presentation featuring several cartoons (including Garfield!) helps students practice this valuable skill. It's a laugh!

http://www.teach-nology.com/worksheets/graphic/bingo5

Bingo! Mark this spot for bingo resources. This site includes a free space in the middle—and everyone wins. Additional resources are available for a small fee, but we found tons of free stuff here!

Name _____

Class _____

What they **SAY.**	What they **MEAN.**

Lifesaver Tool #90.1

Name _____

Class _____

| What they **SAY.** | What they **MEAN.** |

"What does Mama look like, Aunt Queen?" (Draper, p. 32).

Gerald is wondering about his mother and is very anxious about seeing her after many years.

Lifesaver Tool #90.1

Lifesaver Notes

_____

_____

_____

_____

_____

_____

_____

_____

_____

_____

_____

_____

_____

_____

_____

_____

_____

_____

_____

_____

Lifesaver Notes

Chapter 10

Lifesaver Tributes

This "Tribute" section includes shout outs to ten great collaborators. "Sea" their inspirational quotes in Lifesaver Tools #91–100.

Literacy Lifesaver Tribute #91

Rich in Collaboration

Kelly Rich is a fantastic example of a great collaborator. A veteran social studies teacher at Ben Davis High School (Go Giants!), she knows what she wants when she begins a collaborative project. A fan of backwards planning (starting with the end in mind), Kelly comes to the media center with clear objectives, a positive attitude, and a willingness to dive in and get the job done.

Lifesaver Tips

- **Plan ahead.** At our school, library space is limited. When you want to do a big collaborative unit, you need to plan ahead and have an idea of how many days your project will take.

- **Be open-minded.** When I come to the library, I always know what I want to accomplish, but I've learned that there are creative resources and lessons that the library media specialist can add that make the unit even better.

- **Schedule enough time.** It's easier to cancel scheduled days later if the extra time isn't needed, rather than try to add days on to the end of the project that may already be "booked."

- **Ask for help.** Don't be afraid to ask for help when needed. In the case of really rough classes, help with discipline may be necessary. Don't take offense when another adult has to help do crowd control. Remember, you're a team!

- **Grade collaboratively.** At the end of the unit, I always allow an extra day or two to collaborate on grade projects and presentations with the media specialist. It's a great way for the media specialist to get to see the end result (and a little grading help never hurts!).

Lifesaver Text

Social Studies That Sticks by Laurel Schmidt (Heinemann, 2007).

I plan to "stick" with this book a long time—it's the best content-area resource I've seen in a long time!

Lifesaver Trip

http://www.wayne.k12.in.us/bdsocd/sd1.asp

Click on "Mrs. Rich."

Lifesaver Tribute:
Kelly Rich, Social Studies Teacher
Ben Davis High School (Indianapolis, IN)

"Never be afraid to ask for help during a collaborative project. Remember, you're a team!"

Lifesaver Tool #91

Literacy Lifesaver Tribute #92

Coming Up Roses

When Ben Davis High School English Teacher Shannon Rose visits the media center, you can bet that her student projects will always be coming up roses. That's because this veteran teacher uses her creative touch to make her lessons come alive.

Lifesaver Tips

- **Ask the expert.** Always be sure to let the media specialist know what units you're working on. I know what resources I've used in the past, but he or she knows what exciting new ones may have come in that I haven't even seen yet.

- **Project yourself.** I always plan collaborative media center units around a major project. I want students to have something to show for all of their research when they finish. One of my favorite units, for example, is the Renaissance Unit in which the students research stained glass windows and then design and create their own out of tissue paper. We display the projects in the media center at the end of the unit—they make a beautiful display for all to see.

- **Be flexible.** Sometimes the best lesson plans don't work out. When a plan fails, count on your media specialist to help you monitor and adjust as needed.

- **Don't forget to say thanks.** When my classes are in the library, the media specialist works as hard as I do to help my students be successful. At the end of the unit, I always bring the media specialist a cold Diet Coke as a simple way of saying thank you.

- **Picture this!** Don't forget to take pictures of your finished project. The pictures are great to show future students.

Lifesaver Text

Reading Reminders: Tools, Tips and Techniques by Jim Burke (Boynton/Cook, 2000).

This book truly is a lifesaver! Full of student examples, straightforward advice, and ready-to-use reproducibles, this resource is one you won't want to miss!

Lifesaver Trip

http://www.wayne.k12.in.us/bdengd/sd1.asp

Click on "Mrs. Rose."

Lifesaver Tribute:
Shannon Rose, English Teacher
Ben Davis High School (Indianapolis, IN)

"When you finish your collaborative projects, display them in the media center for all to see!"

Lifesaver Tool #92

Literacy Lifesaver Tribute #93

Where's Wendy's Class?

Collaborating on Friendship are Pam Bacon (left) and Wendy Auman.

Where's Wendy's class now? Nearby teachers don't even have to ask anymore. They already know that Wendy Auman and her class are probably at the media center learning their subject matter firsthand. Auman, a veteran teacher at Griggs Road Elementary School (Clover, South Carolina), knows the value of collaboration and shares her expert advice with us.

Lifesaver Tips

- **Be a book worm!** The best way to get students to read is to model reading. During sustained silent reading time, I ignore all the work I have to do and escape into my book. It's critical to show students at an early age that nothing is more important than reading.

- **Tie in to books.** Whenever I can use children's literature to teach a social studies or science concept, I do. My students learn more when we make those connections. The media specialist is wonderful about sending picture books and great content-related novels to me.

- **Time out!** Whenever I can use primary sources to teach my students, I do. My class and I visit the library often and take advantage of all of the materials that extend and enrich the textbooks.

- **Take a break.** I often escape to the media center during my lunch or preparation time. Browsing through the new books or sitting in a quiet corner to read helps me renew and refresh.

- **Book talk.** Ask the media specialist to give booktalks when exciting new books arrive. Leave plenty of time for students to talk about what books they might what to read (or already have!).

Lifesaver Text

Take It to Your Seat Literacy Centers Grades 2–3 by JoEllen Moore (Evan-Moore, 2004).

This series is truly a teacher's survival guide. The lessons are ready-to-use and so portable that they can be done in the classroom, the media center, or even outside!

Lifesaver Trip

http://www.clover2.k12.sc.us/griggs/aboutus/faculty.html

Click on "Wendy Auman (Third Grade)."

Lifesaver Tribute:
Wendy Auman, 3rd-Grade Teacher
Griggs Elementary School (Clover, SC)

"I love my job...I'd never want to do anything else! I'm excited that I can make a difference every day and share my passion for reading!"

Lifesaver Tool #93

Literacy Lifesaver Tribute #94

She's So Witty!

All of Pam's professional books have been dedicated to her friend, media role model, and mentor, Nancy Welch Witty. Nancy is the elementary library media specialist at Rockville Elementary School (Rockville, Indiana). Not only does Nancy have clever, creative ideas guaranteed to hook students on reading, she is one of the most caring people I've ever met. Part of Nancy's success is that she makes every effort to accommodate and work with all patrons and staff in a positive way. As you will see, it's this humble servant attitude that makes others want to line up to she what she's serving up next in the media center!

Lifesaver Tips

- **Be a Cheerleader!** I always make a strong effort to accommodate and work with all patrons of the library in a positive, enthusiastic way—especially instructional staff. I respond to *any* idea, problem, or project that is presented to me with, "YES! Let's try it!"

- **YHBA!** The Village People may not be singing "YHBA," but readers who love great books will! I always implement the "Young Hoosier Book Award" contest each year. It works especially well with primary grade teachers because I know they are reading aloud twenty high-quality books. The intermediate teachers often read aloud two to five YHBA chapter books to their classes. I can't say enough about the benefits of reading aloud to kids!

- **Check in "Periodically."** Dialogue among teachers and myself is so beneficial. For example, this summer I revamped my annual periodical order, because together as a staff we have determined the need to get our boy population on board for recreational reading. We're going to start to meet that goal through high-interest magazines.

- **Do It the "Write" Way!** Use journals whenever you can as part of your library lessons to get students writing down their feelings and responding to great books!

- **My best advice?** Tailor your basic role as a library media specialist according to one of my favorite poems (which I often share with my students, who love it too!):

My Favorite Word

There is one word~
My favorite~
The very, very best.
It isn't no or maybe.
It's YES, YES, YES, YES, YES!

"Yes, Yes, you may" and
"Yes, of course," and
"Yes, please help yourself."
And when I want a piece of cake,
"Why, yes, it's on the shelf!"

Some candy? "Yes!"
A cookie? "Yes!"
A movie? "Yes, we'll go!"

I love it when they say my word:
YES, YES, YES, YES! (Not no!)

—by Lucia and James Hymes

Author's Note: You see what I mean? Nancy's positive attitude and wonderful spirit are a blessing to those around her. Thanks for being such an inspiration, Nancy! —PB

Lifesaver Text

The Read-Aloud Handbook (6th ed.) by Jim Trelease (Penguin, 2006).

Lifesaver Trip

http://www.rockville.k12.in.us

Click on "Staff Directory," and "N. Witty."

Lifesaver Tribute:
Nancy Welch Witty, Library Media Specialist
Rockville Elementary School (Rockville, IN)

"I respond to ANY idea, problem or project that is presented to me with a positive and resounding 'Yes!'"

Lifesaver Tool #94

Literacy Lifesaver Tribute #95

Here's Harvey!

Say the words "Carl A. Harvey II" around Indiana (and soon the world!) and the picture of an outstanding educator and professional media specialist immediately springs to mind. Carl is the library media specialist at North Elementary School (Noblesville, Indiana). Pam had the opportunity to be around Carl personally only a few times, but every time I walk away more energized and inspired. Carl's truly a tribute to the profession. Luckily, we were able to steal a few moments from his busy schedule to get some advice! By the way, Carl was too humble to mention it, but I have to shout his praises here. He and his school were awarded the coveted National School Library Media Program of the Year in 2007. Wow!

Lifesaver Tips

- **It's All about Collaboration.** I have the opportunity to work at an amazing school where collaboration is central to all we do. Each grade level plans together weekly (including the library media specialist and resource teachers). We organize opportunities to talk across grade levels about data and instruction. We work together to keep consistency throughout our building for student behavior and expectations. This is truly a school where we are one big family that works together to provide our students with the best learning opportunities possible.

- **Become an Essential Instructional Partner.** This supportive, collaborative environment allows the library media program to be essential to instruction. Not only do we provide resources and materials to support teaching literacy, but I'm a part of the development of curriculum, instruction, and assessment.

- **Make Connections.** We are constantly making connections among library media, technology, and the curriculum. We interweave it all together to give students rich learning opportunities.

- **Work Together.** Working together, we are all on the same path in the journey, and we're all there to help and support each other. We (teachers, parents, students, administrators) take all of our strengths and utilize them to be most effective—and then we take our weaknesses to help each other become even better.

- **Be Persistent.** When collaborating with teachers, it is important to always throw out ideas and suggestions of possible collaborative connections. It just takes the right idea to hook a teacher to collaborate with the media specialist, so even when they turn down the opportunity, keep at it. The right idea will come eventually!

Author's Note: Wow! I want to work at his school! —PB

Lifesaver Texts

Assessing Learning: Librarians and Teachers as Partners by Violet Harada and Joan Yoshina (Libraries Unlimited, 2005).

Building Influence for the School Librarian: Tenets, Targets, and Tactics by Gary Hartzell (Linworth Publishing, 2003).

The Power of Reading (2nd ed.) by Steven Krashen (Libraries Unlimited, 2004).

Lifesaver Trip

http://www.carl-harvey.com

Be sure to check out the picture of Carl as a toddler pulling books off of the library shelf. I guess wanting to reshelve was always a part of his future goals!

Lifesaver Tribute:
Carl A. Harvey II, Library Media Specialist
North Elementary School (Noblesville, IN)

"Often the door to collaboration can be opened when the media specialist brings something to the table which the classroom teacher is unfamiliar or unsure about, but has to do with their curriculum. It could be a topic they don't enjoy teaching...or it could be a requirement to use technology in instruction or student projects. Use this as the hook to help that teacher and open the door to collaborative projects."

Lifesaver Tool #95

Literacy Lifesaver Tribute #96

Go Geilfuss!

I've "met" Tom Geilfuss only recently, thanks to the powers of the Internet. When I sent out a plea for responses from teachers who believe in the power of collaboration with the library media specialist, Tom was first to answer the call. Tom is a collaborator working in the education field from Milwaukee, Wisconsin, who has been inspired by the works of Carol Kulthau and believes, from firsthand experience, in the power of collaboration. Thanks for your perspective, Tom!

Lifesaver Tips

- **Collaboration Is Key!** Collaboration is the key to successful research projects. When I planned with the librarian, we worked as equal partners from the beginning of the project to the end of the project.

- **Be Equal Partners.** Throughout the collaborative process, we both knew what kinds of materials the students would need. We both knew what kinds of information search strategies we would need to use. We both knew which of us would cover what in mini-lessons about the various parts of the research process. We both knew simply that we were equal partners and treated each other as such.

- **Plan Ahead to Avoid Pitfalls.** The library media specialist knew what background knowledge the students had from our previous work in the classroom. We decided together on what graphic organizers would be helpful to get the kids over likely stumbling blocks in the research process. Most importantly, there were two teachers to help during class time in the library media center to assist individual students with their specific questions and research problems.

- **Chime In.** When I gave a short presentation in the media center, the librarian would often add ideas or suggestions I had overlooked, and vice versa.

- **Rely on Your Partner's Expertise.** The librarian was able to find quality Web sites and post links to these on our library Web site so that students would not spend an inordinate amount of time in Google land. The librarian also provided essential print resources they could use in their research.

Lifesaver Text

Reading the Web by Maya B. Eagleton and Elizabeth Dobler (Guilford Press, 2007).

Lifesaver Trip

http://www.usmk12.org/display/router.aspx

Click on "About Us," then "Faculty and Administration," then "Geilfuss, Thomas."

Lifesaver Tribute:
Tom Geilfuss, Educator
University School of Milwaukee
(River Hills, WI)

"Collaboration is key to successful research projects. Collaboration allowed each of us [the teacher & media specialist] to help individual kids with their specific questions or research problems."

Lifesaver Tool #96

Literacy Lifesaver Tribute #97

Cook's Choice!

Collaborating on their suntans are Tammy Bacon (left) and Anna Cook (right).

Collaborating on friendship and reading are Tammy and Anna's daughters, Bailey and Alexandra.

Anna Cook has a heart for collaboration and a passion for literacy. She is the coordinator for special programs and literacy for the Metropolitan School District of Decatur Township and has extensive experience in the area of staff development and grant writing. She truly has a gift for multitasking and meeting numerous demands—both personally and professionally.

Lifesaver Tips

- **Build personal relationships.** This has a huge impact on the quality of your collaboration.

- **Make time for reflection.** The power of reflection is key to learning. When you are taking on a new challenge, it is more important than ever to reflect and learn from your experience.

- **Keep an open mind.** It is really important to be flexible and open-minded when working with people with varied personalities and strengths.

- **Conversation is key.** Communication is a powerful vehicle for learning!

- **Keep it fun!** Don't be afraid to laugh at yourself!

Lifesaver Text

Power Up! Building Reading Strength by Roger Farr (Steck-Vaughn, 2004).

Anna says, "Dr. Farr has had a huge impact on my beliefs in the area of reading and writing."

Lifesaver Trip

http://www.msddecatur.k12.in.us

Click on "Administration" and "Curriculum and Instruction."

Lifesaver Tribute:
Anna Cook, Special Programs Coordinator, MSD Decatur Township (Indianapolis, IN)

"Keep collaboration fun and don't be afraid to laugh at yourself!"

Lifesaver Tool #97

Literacy Lifesaver Tribute #98

Give Callahan a Hand!

"Sea" Diana and Tammy collaborate as literacy coordinators.

Diana Callahan is the primary literacy coordinator at Deer Meadow Primary in Greencastle, Indiana. Her knowledge of literacy learning and theory is extensive, and she is intentional and prescriptive when working with both students and teachers. She credits collaboration for totally changing classrooms. Her belief is that it takes many staff members working together to meet the individual needs of our students: teacher to teacher, literacy coordinator to teacher, teacher to special education teacher, teacher to media specialist, teacher to special area teachers, and so on. She models the importance of this collaboration in formal and informal ways throughout her busy day!

Lifesaver Tips

- **Don't be afraid of disequilibrium.** This shows that change is taking place and that people are moving forward.

- **Make time for communication.** The power of communication is vital to collaboration that affects student achievement.

- **Be willing to step outside your comfort zone.** It is important to model this for staff and students.

- **Extend welcome and presume welcome!** Remind staff members of these important tenets to consider at the beginning of each training session. It sets the tone for positive collaboration!

- **Share ownership!** Classroom teachers must open the door and allow others in!

Lifesaver Text

Tools of the Mind by Elena Bodrova and Debora Leong (Prentice Hall, 2006).

Diana says, "Vygotsky's theory has had a powerful influence on my beliefs of teaching and learning."

Lifesaver Trip

http://www.greencastle.k12.in.us

Click on "Deer Meadow."

Lifesaver Tribute:
Diana Callahan, Literacy Coordinator
Deer Meadow Primary
(Greencastle, IN)

Meet Me at the Edge

"...Where I stand with my feet planted in what I can do best on my own.

... Where I can taste and test new discoveries, moving toward growth and greater boundaries.

... Where you will teach me, support me—with great diligence at first—gradually releasing me as the new discovery becomes a confident old friend.

Meet me at the edge of my understanding, becoming my bridge to new success."

Diana Callahan

Lifesaver Tool #98

Morris Matters

Gwen Morris is the principal of Deer Meadow Primary School in Greencastle, Indiana. Her passion for literacy and staff development is a true tribute to her commitment to lifelong learning. She believes that literacy is the heart of learning and that children must have this foundation to make it in other core subjects. She continuously models that everyone shares in the responsibility to attain the success of each child.

Lifesaver Tips

- **Work at collaboration.** Collaboration must be job-embedded.

- **Buy in!** All stakeholders must believe in the process.

- **Make it meaningful.** Collaboration must be meaningful and important to have a positive impact on student achievement.

- **Data drives instruction.** Student assessment data must drive instructional decision making. Collaboration is the vehicle for sharing this information.

- **Collaboration must be comprehensive.** Collaboration must cross grade levels, schools, and administrators and include the total school community.

Lifesaver Texts

Invitations by Reggie Routman (Heinemann, 1994).

Guided Reading by Irene Fountas and Gay Sy Pinnell (Heinemann, 1996).

Lifesaver Trip

http://www.greencastle.k12.in.us

Click on "Deer Meadow Primary."

Lifesaver Tribute:
Gwen Morris, Principal
Deer Meadow Primary
(Greencastle, IN)

"Collaboration must drive data interpretation to have a positive impact on student achievement."

Lifesaver Tool #99

Literacy Lifesaver Tribute #100

Kelley's Keys to Collaboration

Mrs. Kay Kelley

Kay Kelley is a primary literacy coordinator and T-1 transition teacher for Nappanee Elementary in Warsaw, Indiana. Her dynamic personality, enthusiasm for learning, and passion for literacy are just a few of her many strengths. As a literacy coordinator, she models collaborative strategies through her work as a writing coach and effective teacher.

Lifesaver Tips

Kelly says, "I define 'literacy' when I look at a sapling, struggling to survive despite nature's uncertainties. With perseverance, the sapling grows into a majestic tree, towering above all others and stretching its branches in every direction. We, as parents and teachers, must nurture our youngest readers by creating an insatiable yearning for knowledge and pleasure, found only in literature."

- **Be perseverant.**

- **Team with parents.**

- **Nurture our youngest readers.**
- **Create a yearning for knowledge.**
- **Keep the passion for literacy.**

Lifesaver Texts

About the Authors by Lisa Cleaveland and Katie Wood Ray (Heinemann, 2004).

Reading with Meaning by Debbie Miller (Stenhouse, 2002).

The Daily Five by Gail Boushey and Joan Moser (Stenhouse, 2006).

Lifesaver Trip

http://www.wanee.org

Click on "Our Schools" and "Nappanee Elementary."

Lifesaver Tribute:
Kay Kelley, Literacy Coordinator,
T-1 Transition Teacher
Nappanee Elementary
(Warsaw, IN)

"With increased accountability in our assessment driven times, we must remain firmly "planted" in our passion for literacy."

Lifesaver Tool #100.1

Lifesaver Notes

_____
_____
_____
_____
_____
_____
_____
_____
_____
_____
_____
_____
_____
_____
_____
_____
_____
_____
_____
_____
_____

Glossary

Educational Terms

Blog. Short for weblog, a blog is an Internet journal intended for public viewing.

Bloom's Taxonomy. A theory of learning developed by educational psychologist Benjamin Bloom that is widely used in educational circles.

Genre. A type of book or literature (e.g., fiction, nonfiction, romance, mystery).

Formative assessment. A means to assess learning. A pre-test is a type of formative assessment.

Lexile. A mathematical formula used to determine the reading level or difficulty of a text.

Mnemonic device. A technique to help us remember information. Example: to remember the proper spelling of "principal," we might tell students that "Your principal is your "pal."

Rubric. A guideline to assist in scoring an assignment.

Scribe. A person who writes down information for another; a recorder.

Summative assessment. An assessment given at the end of a lesson or unit. Summative assessments are often used for data collection purposes.

Educational Strategies

Fishbowl technique. A type of learning that takes place as the audience observes a lesson or activity demonstrated by participants in the middle of the room (i.e., observers are outside looking in).

Jigsaw technique. A type of learning in which individual teams (or students) are given one part of a much larger text to present to the whole group. This technique is useful when time is short and much material needs to be covered.

Kagan cooperative learning. A team-building approach developed by Spencer Kagan in which students work together in different "structures" to achieve a common goal.

Knee-to-knee technique. An information-sharing strategy in which students share information with the person directly across from them.

Pick a partner. An information-sharing strategy in which students choose their own partner but are not limited by the partner's proximity (as in the knee-to-knee technique).

Shoulder partner. An information-sharing strategy in which students can choose a partner at their left shoulder or right shoulder to engage in discussion.

Turn-and-talk technique. A way to share information in which students choose a nearby partner to engage in discussion.

References

Anderson, Laurie Halse. 2006. *Speak.* New York: Penguin Group.

Arthur, T. S. 2007. *Danger.* Charleston, SC: BiblioBazaar.

Bodrova, Elena, and Debora Leong. 2006. *Tools of the Mind: The Vygotskian Approach to Early Childhood Education.* Upper Saddle River, NJ: Prentice Hall.

Boushey, Gail, and Joan Moser. 2006. *The Daily Five: Fostering Literacy Independence in the Elementary Grades.* Portland, ME: Stenhouse.

Brown, Margaret Wise. 1990. *The Important Book.* New York: HarperCollins.

Burke, Jim. 2000. *Reading Reminders: Tools, Tips and Techniques.* Portsmouth, NH: Boynton/Cook.

Burns, Bonnie. 2001. *Guided Reading.* Thousand Oaks, CA: Sage.

Buzzeo, Toni, and Jane Kurtz. 1999. *Teriffic Connections with Authors, Illustrators, and Storytellers: Real Space and Virtual Links.* Englewood, CO: Libraries Unlimited.

Cleaveland, Lisa, and Katie Wood Ray. 2004. *About the Authors: Writing Workshop with Our Youngest Writers.* Portsmouth, NH: Heinemann.

Codell, Esme. 2003. *How to Get Your Child to Love Reading: For Ravenous and Reluctant Readers Alike.* Chapel Hill, NC: Algonquin Books.

DeGroat, Diane. 2003. *Liar, Liar, Pants on Fire.* San Francisco: Chronicle Books.

Draper, Sharon M. 1996. *Tears of a Tiger.* New York: Simon Pulse.

Draper, Sharon M. 1998. *Forged by Fire.* New York: Simon & Schuster Children's Publishing.

Draper, Sharon M. 2002. *Darkness Before Dawn.* New York: Simon & Schuster Children's Publishing.

Draper, Sharon M. 2006. *Ziggy and the Black Dinosaurs.* New York: Simon & Schuster.

Eagleton, Maya, and Elizabeth Dobler. 2007. *Reading the Web.* New York: Guilford Press.

Ehlert, Lois. 1991. *Red Leaf, Yellow Leaf.* San Diego, CA: Harcourt Children's Books.

Farr, Roger. 2004. *Power Up! Building Reading Strength*. Orlando, FL: Steck-Vaughn.

Fitzgerald, F. Scott. 2004. *The Great Gatsby*. New York: Simon & Schuster.

Fountas, Irene C. and Gay Su Pinnell. 1996. *Guided Reading: Good First Teaching for All Children*. Portsmouth, NH: Heinemann.

Frost, Helen. 2007. *Keesha's House*. New York: Farrar, Straus and Giroux.

Frost, Helen. 2008. *Monarch and Milkweed*. New York: Simon & Schuster Children's Publishing.

Harada, Violet, and Joan Yoshina. 2005. *Assessing Learning: Librarians and Teachers as Partners*. Englewood, CO: Libraries Unlimited.

Hartzell, Gary. 2003. *Building Influence for the School Librarian: Tenets, Targets and Tactics*. Columbus, OH: Linworth.

Harvey, Stephanie, and Anne Goudvis. 2007. *Strategies That Work: Teaching Comprehension for Understanding and Engagement*. Portland, ME: Stenhouse Publishers.

Hoyt, Linda. 2006. *Interactive Read Alouds*. Portsmouth, NH: FirstHand.

Jenkins, Steve. 2004. *Hottest, Coldest, Highest, Deepest*. Boston: Houghton Mifflin.

Korman, Gordon. 2003. *The Discovery: Dive #1*. New York: Scholastic.

Korman, Gordon. 2006. *The Ultimate Nose Picker Collection*. New York: Hyperion Books.

Krashen, Steven. 2004. *The Power of Reading* (2nd ed.). Englewood, CO: Libraries Unlimited.

Lovell, Patty, and David Catrow. 2001. *Stand Tall, Molly Lou Melon*. New York: Penguin Young Readers Group.

Mannis, Celeste Davidson. 2002. *One Leaf Rides the Wind*. New York: Viking.

Miller, Debbie. 2002. *Reading with Meaning: Teaching Comprehension in the Primary Grades*. Portland, ME: Stenhouse.

Moore, JoEllen. 2004. *Take It to Your Seat Literacy Centers Grades 2–3*. Monterey, CA: Evan-Moore.

Myers, Walter Dean. 2005. *Shooter*. New York: HarperCollins.

Parrish, Peggy. 2003. *Amelia Bedilia Collection*. New York: HarperTrophy.

Peters, Lisa Westberg. 1996. *October Smiled Back*. New York: Henry Holt.

Rennison, Louise. 1999. *Angus, Thongs and Full-Frontal Snogging*. New York: HarperTeen.

Rennison, Louise. 2001. *On the Bright Side, I'm Now the Girlfriend of a Sex God*. New York: HarperTeen.

Rennison, Louise. 2001. *Knocked Out by My Nunga-Nungas*. New York: HarperTeen.

Rennison, Louise. 2002. *Dancing in My Nuddy-Pants*. New York: HarperTeen.

Rennison, Louise. 2004. *Away Laughing on a Fast Camel*. New York: HarperTeen.

Rennison, Louise. 2005. *Then He Ate My Boy Entrancers*. New York: HarperTeen.

Rennison, Louise. 2006. *Startled by His Furry Shorts*. New York: HarperTeen.

Rennison, Louise. 2007. *Love Is a Many Trousered Thing*. New York: HarperTeen.

Rennison, Louise. 2008. *Stop in the Name of Pants*. New York: HarperTeen.

Routman, Regie. 1994. *Invitations: Changing as Teachers and Learners*. Portsmouth, NH: Heinemann.

Schmidt, Laurel. 2007. *Social Studies That Sticks*. Portsmouth, NH: Heinemann.

Steinbeck, John. 1993. *Of Mice and Men*. New York: Penguin Group.

Trelease, Jim. 2006. *The Read-Aloud Handbook* (6th ed.). New York: Penguin.

Index

ABOUT THE AUTHORS

PAMELA S. BACON has spent seventeen years in education—thirteen years in the media specialist role (K–12) and four years as a reading teacher (7–12). She has a Master's Degree in Education and a certification in reading instruction. She is the author of three professional books for Libraries Unlimited and more than twenty magazine articles.

TAMMY K. BACON has spent twenty years in education—five years as an elementary teacher and fifteen years as a principal and literacy coach. She holds a Master's Degree in Administration and a certification in literacy coaching.